Reason Within the
Bounds of Religion

Reason Within the Bounds of Religion
Second Edition

by
Nicholas Wolterstorff

William B. Eerdmans Publishing Company
Grand Rapids, Michigan

Copyright © 1976, 1984 by Wm. B. Eerdmans Publishing Co.
255 Jefferson Avenue S.E., Grand Rapids, Michigan 49503

Printed in the United States of America

First published 1976. Second Edition 1984

Reprinted, October 1993

Library of Congress Cataloging in Publication Data

Wolterstorff, Nicholas.
    Reason within the bounds of religion.

    1. Belief and doubt—Addresses, essays, lectures. 2. Theory
(Philosophy)—Addresses, essays, lectures. 3. Philosophy and
religion—Addresses, essays, lectures. 4. Thought and thinking
—Addresses, essays, lectures. I. Title.
BD215.W65   215   76-7514
ISBN 0-8028-1643-6

To one Harry and two Henrys—Jellema, Stob, Zylstra—who twenty-five years ago first gave me a vision of what it is to be a Christian scholar

Contents

Preface to the Second Edition

The first edition of this book comprised only what stands here as Part I. Today, some seven years after the composition of this Part, I could not write it in the same way. I continue to stand behind the main line of argument. But today, after seven years of continuing reflection on the issues here raised (some of this provoked by responses to the book) I would not only want to correct some points and forestall some misunderstandings but, more importantly, I would feel compelled to discuss the issues more elaborately, with more explanations, qualifications, refinements, etc. I judge, though, that the original book's comparatively stark presentation of the issues remains of use; it has the virtue of walking right past most of the interesting trees so as to see the woods whole. Hence I have decided to allow it to be published unchanged.

What I have done instead is add a second part. Two fundamental issues face all scholars. They must decide which matters to investigate. And on the matters under investigation, they must decide which views to hold. In the first edition of this book, I addressed myself exclusively to the bearing of the

Christian faith on the latter of these two issues. In the new Part II, I address myself to the bearing of the Christian faith on the former. The material now contained in Part II originally appeared in *Christian Scholar's Review* (9 [1980], 317–34) and is reprinted here with their permission.

N.P.W.

Preface to the First Edition

The following is a tract for Christians. I welcome others to listen in. But Christians are the ones I am writing for.

What I have written for them is a soliloquy of sorts. I ask what my own fundamental identity as a Christian has to do with my practice of scholarship and, more importantly, what it *ought* to have to do with it.

There is not much conversation embedded in the soliloquy. Many other Christian scholars have reflected on the relation of their religious commitment to their scholarship. I have read a good many of those—agreeing often, disagreeing perhaps more often, all the while profiting. But I have decided here to speak my own piece and leave the detailed conversation with those fellow inquirers for some other occasion.

The general topic under consideration is religion and science (*Wissenschaft*). And though it is from within the Christian religion that I address the topic, the *structure* of my answer would hold for other religions as well. To the convinced Buddhist I would say that integrity requires that he use his religious beliefs as control within his devising and weighing of theories—an obvious counterpart of what I say to Christians.

I am a philosopher, and my topic is a philosophical one. So the soliloquy will be philosophical. Yet I have written in the hope that persons other than philosophers will find it comprehensible and illuminating. It does not presuppose any philosophical expertise. It may be, however, that some readers who lack contact with the manner of philosophers will find Sections 5 and 6 tough going. Nothing of indispensable importance will be lost if they simply skip over those sections. For the benefit of those familiar with philosophy I have appended some rather elaborate footnotes. My title is, as philosophy students may recognize, freely borrowed from Kant.

The reader will discover that the essay is somewhat episodic as regards the connection between sections. This has been deliberate. As the reader goes through the essay he should not be unduly concerned to spy the connections between the sections. By the time he is finished the connections will be apparent.

The substance of this essay was originally given in the form of lectures to the faculties of those colleges which are members of the Consortium of Colleges in the Reformed and Presbyterian Tradition. I hereby extend to them my thanks for their support and critique. And as is true for much of what I publish, I am deeply indebted to my colleagues in the philosophy department at Calvin College for suggestions and criticisms.

N.P.W.

Part I
FAITH AND THEORY

1/ Some historical examples of control beliefs

On February 19, 1616, the Holy Office in Rome submitted to its theological experts the following two propositions for their assessment:

> **1. The sun is the center of the world and hence immovable of local motion.**
> **2. The earth is not the center of the world, nor immovable, but moves according to the whole of itself, also with a diurnal motion.**

The theologians met four days later on February 23, and the day after that announced the results of their deliberations. Their conclusions were unanimous. The first proposition they declared to be "foolish and absurd philosophically, and formally heretical, inasmuch as it expressly contradicts the doctrine of the Holy Scripture in many passages, both in their literal meaning and according to the general interpretation of the Fathers and Doctors." The second proposition they declared "to receive the same censure in philosophy, and as regards theological truth to be at least erroneous in faith."

The matter was then handed over to the Congregation of the Index (under the General Congregation of the Inquisition). On March 5 of the same year this Congregation handed down its decree:

> It has . . . come to the knowledge of the said Congregation that the Pythagorean doctrine—which is false and altogether opposed to the Holy Scripture—of the motion of the Earth, and the immobility of the Sun, which is also taught by Nicolaus Copernicus in *De revolutionibus orbium coelestium*, and by Diego de Zuñiga (in the book) on Job, is now being spread abroad and accepted by many. . . . Therefore, in order that this opinion may not insinuate itself any further to the prejudice of Catholic faith, the Holy Congregation has decreed that the said Nicolaus Copernicus' *De revolutionibus orbium*, and Diego de Zuñiga's *On Job*, be suspended until they be corrected. . . . In witness whereof the present decree has been signed and sealed with the hands and with the seal of the most eminent and Reverend Lord Cardinal of St. Cecilia, Bishop of Albano, on the fifth day of March, 1616.

So much for the record of the most famous instance of the Church's scrutiny of the affairs of natural science.[1] Though his name is never mentioned in the passages cited above, it was Galileo who had instigated this whole affair by his defense of the Copernican theory of the motion of the heavenly bodies against the Ptolemaic theory. After reflecting on the matter, the officials of the Church judged that the theory was philosophically—that is, scientifically—absurd. More important (they were, after all, not a

Royal Academy of Science), they judged that the theory contradicted the Holy Scriptures, which they regarded as authoritatively true. Their belief in the authoritative truth of the Holy Scriptures functioned as a *control* over the scientific theories which they were willing to accept. Likewise, the specific things that they interpreted the Holy Scriptures as saying functioned thus. Because the Copernican theory violated their control beliefs they rejected it. A classic case of the refusal to allow to science* its free, untrammelled, autonomous, rational progress, is it not?

Let us see.

Less than a century after those deliberations a new dispute wracked the physics of the Western world. Copernicus by now was accepted: the earth moved around the sun, no doubt about it. What was now at the center of inquiry and dispute were the general laws concerning the motion of heavenly and terrestrial bodies. In the first half of the century Descartes had proposed the speculative mechanistic thesis that matter can be moved only by the motion of contiguous matter, that there can be no action at a distance. The physical universe consists not of lumps of matter sprinkled thinly throughout empty space and acting on each other across the void, but of solid

------

*When I use the word "science" in the following pages, I shall always mean by it the academic disciplines—what the Germans call *Wissenschaft*.

peas of matter floating in a thin soup of ether. The Cartesians saw this vision as freeing them from the "fruitless speculations" of the medieval scientists, who held that all things by their nature seek to come to rest, those with gravity seeking their rest downward and those with levity seeking it upward. With this vision before them the Cartesians set out on a research program designed to discover the detailed mechanistic laws governing the motion of matter.

Then in 1687 Newton published his *Principia,* with its theory of universal gravitational attraction. The Cartesians at once went on the attack, accusing Newton of reintroducing obscurantist medieval ideas of essences and natures. They emphasized the counter-evidence to the Newtonian theory, which they regarded as confirmation of the theory's fundamentally defective character; and they searched for ways to handle the counter-evidence to their own.[2] In this case we see someone's *philosophical* beliefs functioning as a control over the scientific theories he is willing to accept. But now it is the scientists rather than some clerics whose beliefs function thus. Their control beliefs govern their actual scientific work. Is it possible that scientists themselves can impede the free, untrammelled, autonomous, rational progress of science?

Let us once again take a leap, this time over a bit more than two centuries, to the great physicist Ernst Mach. It was Mach's belief that the task of the natural scientist is to find simple and regular connections between the elements of reality. His inclination was to regard these elements as sensations. Apparently he viewed this as an ontological *hypothesis,* susceptible to criticism. Methodologically, however, it functioned for him as a touchstone, for he appended to it the principle that natural science should contain only concepts which can be connected with sensations. Since neither the atomic theory of his own day nor the Newtonian theory of absolute space stood up to this requirement, he rejected them and went on to explore how physics might be reconstructed on a sensationalistic basis. To Max Planck's charge that his proposals diverged too far from the actual structure of natural science Mach replied that science had become a church, and that he had no intention of being a member of a church, scientific or otherwise. If necessary, he would renounce the very title of 'scientist.' *"Die Gedankenfreiheit ist mir lieber,"* he said: "freedom of thought is more dear to me."[3]

In Mach's case, again, a philosophical belief—here a somewhat tentatively held ontological vision—functioned as a control within the practice of science, determining the rejection of a variety of theories and requiring alternative lines of thought for its positive elaboration. And now how do we put our question? Who in this mélange was impeding the free, untrammelled, autonomous, rational progress of science?

The logical positivists of the 1920s and 1930s held that observation was the solid foundation of all knowledge. Most of them regarded this as settled truth rather than tentative hypothesis. And all of them differed from Mach in believing that natural science *as it is* is a specimen of knowledge. They did not seek a critique and restructuring of natural science *à la* Mach, but a logical analysis exhibiting the connection of the whole scientific superstructure with its observational base. They failed, and the tale thereof has oft been told.[4] But confronted with their failure they did not follow through on their empiricist conviction and toss out that in natural science which is not grounded in observation. Instead they kept their troth to natural science and surrendered their empiricist convictions along with their program of logical analysis.

Here, then, we have an interesting reversal. The positivists used the conviction that the body of natural science is quite all right as it is, as a control within their philosophical activities. It led them to the rejection of certain theories and to the search for alternatives. Natural science rather than philosophy here plays the part of the demanding mistress. But the faith which the positivists displayed in natural science was not itself arrived at scientifically. On the contrary, it resembles in striking ways the confidence of the Congregation of the Inquisition in the veracity of Holy Scripture.

2/ *The question posed*

The Christian who is a scholar finds himself in two communities: the community of his fellow Christians and the community of his fellow scholars. Each has its own criteria for membership, its own characteristic practices, its own characteristic beliefs, its own characteristic training programs. Without a doubt a person can simply live in the two different communities, doing as the Athenians do when in Athens and as the Jerusalemites when in Jerusalem. But if one who is a scholar as well as a Christian wants coherence in life—or even if he only wants self-understanding—he cannot help asking, how does my membership in these two communities fit together? That is what I shall ask in the following pages.

Part of my answer to this question will involve sketching out some elements of a theory of theorizing.[5] The basic issue behind our question is that of the role of one's Christian commitment in one's practice of scholarship. To be sure, though there is much more to the practice of scholarship than accepting and rejecting theories (and thus a good deal more whose connection to Christian commitment deserves exploration) certainly this is central. Consequently, it is a theory of theorizing that we need, along with an understanding of the nature of Christian commitment.

I must emphasize that what follows is only a *sketch* of some *elements* of a theory of theorizing, not a full-fledged theory. At best what I shall offer are suggestions for a research program which if carried out would yield a full-fledged theory. My goal is not to present a finished product but rather to propose a promising line of attack.

I do not wish to leave the impression that I am ignoring theories of theorizing which have been proposed in the past to Christian scholars for their acceptance. I do not see myself as a lonely pioneer on the far side of the mountains from civilization. In the twentieth century especially Herman Dooyeweerd has seen the need for such a theory and has tried to construct one. Yet though I have learned from proposals of other Christians along these lines all such theories as I am acquainted with seem to me either to misconstrue the nature of theoretical inquiry or of Christian commitment or (most commonly) at crucial junctures to substitute rhetoric and metaphor for the close analysis that is required. It is often said, for instance, that everyone has a "set of presuppositions" or a "perspective on reality" to bring to a theoretical inquiry. That may be true. But saying such things cannot be the end of the matter. It must at best be the beginning.

3/ *Radical harmonizing*

The logical positivist pledged his troth to science.
Curiously, in subtle fashion many contemporary
Christian thinkers do the same.

Repeatedly since the ultimate victory of Copernicus over the Congregation of the Inquisition,
theologians and ordinary Christians have been
forced to yield their ground and beat an embarrassed
retreat. First it was before the onslaught of the
heliocentric theory of planetary motion; then it was
before that of the theory of evolution; then it was
before that of textual-critical theories about the origins of Scripture.

Convinced that this resistance/retreat pattern was
a mistake a number of twentieth-century Christian
thinkers have aimed to construe authentic Christian
commitment and its relation to science in such a way
that there could in principle be no conflict between
commitment and science. Science tells us (say)
about the empirical facts. Authentic commitment
pertains to—well, *something else*. Accordingly science cannot possibly put commitment on the defensive. Where there can be no attack there need be no

defense. By the same token, commitment cannot possibly put science on the defensive. Christian commitment cannot yield a *critique* of science.

Underlying this approach is thus a fundamental *conformism* with respect to science. Science—at least from the standpoint of authentic Christian commitment—is and always will be all right just as it is. In that way these contemporary Christian thinkers are brothers beneath the skin with the logical positivists.

It would distract us from our main purpose to canvass even the dominant strategies adopted for this purpose. But to give some feeling for the point let me explain one of the best known attempts along this line, R. M. Hare's theory of what he fetchingly calls *bliks*.

Hare formulated his theory in response to a lecture by Anthony Flew which contended that if one scrutinizes how people guard their religious convictions one sees that they treat them as compatible with the happening of anything whatsoever. In other words, these beliefs are not falsifiable. And because they are not falsifiable they do not constitute genuine assertions. They make no claims on actuality.

Now since the time of Flew's lecture it has repeatedly been remarked by philosophers and historians of science that scientists convinced of the truth of some scientific theory behave exactly the way Flew says religious believers do.[6] Accordingly, if Flew's argument were a good one, we would conclude that convinced scientists do not assert anything either. And then one is led to wonder when human beings do assert things—only when they are not convinced?

But Hare responded differently. To Flew's conclusions that religious commitment does not involve holding certain propositions to be true, and that to express one's commitment is not to make any assertion, Hare pleaded *nolo contendere*. By regarding Flew's argument for this as decisive, he surrendered the entire field of facts and of the assertion of facts to the scientist. Religious commitment, on the other hand, consists in having a distinctive *blik* on the world.

To make more or less clear what he means by *blik*, Hare says the following:

> A certain lunatic is convinced that all dons want to murder him. His friends introduce him to all the mildest and most respectable dons that they can find, and after each of them has retired, they say, "You see, he doesn't really want to murder you; he spoke to you in a most cordial manner; surely you are convinced now?" But the lunatic replies, "Yes, but that was only his diabolical cunning; he's really plotting against me the whole time, like the rest of them; I know it, I tell you." However many kindly dons are produced, the reaction is still the same.
>
> Now we say that such a person is deluded. But what is he deluded about? About the truth or falsity of an assertion? Let us apply Flew's test to him. There is no behavior of dons that can be enacted which he will accept as counting against his theory; and therefore his theory, on this test,

asserts nothing. But it does not follow that there is no difference between what he thinks about dons and what most of us think about them—otherwise we should not call him a lunatic and ourselves sane, and dons would have no reason to feel uneasy about his presence in Oxford.

Let us call that in which we differ from this lunatic, our respective *bliks*. He has an insane *blik* about dons; we have a sane one. It is important to realize that we have a sane one, not no *blik* at all; for there must be two sides to any argument—if he has a wrong *blik*, then those who are right about dons must have a right one.

It was Hume who taught us that our whole commerce with the world depends upon our *blik* about the world; and that differences between *bliks* about the world cannot be settled by observation of what happens in the world. That was why, having performed the interesting experiment of doubting the ordinary man's *blik* about the world, and showing that no proof could be given to make us adopt one *blik* rather than another, he turned to backgammon to take his mind off the problem.[7]

If Hare's *blik* theory is meant to be about actual Christian commitment, he is surely mistaken. People sometimes do surrender their Christian commitments. Usually they do so because of conflict between their Christian commitment and what they have come to believe from some other source. Often in our culture that other source is a development in science. A person's Christian commitment constantly runs the risk of coming into conflict with his science, and his science constantly runs the risk of coming into conflict with his Christian commitment. We must explore how and why revisions occur when such conflict emerges. The claim that no such revisions ever occur because no such conflict ever emerges is utterly false.

But Hare is probably discussing how things ought to go, not how they do go. It is likely that he is recommending tacitly that Christians revise their commitment in such a way that no such conflict can ever emerge. If that is so, he is engaged in a classic strategy: trying to harmonize Christian commitment with science. In his case he is doing so by recommending the radical device of revising commitment in such a way that in principle no conflict between the two can ever arise. Whether Christian commitment *can* or *should* be thus revised is a matter to be taken up later. The only point here is that Hare's harmonizing proposal amounts to a radical conformism with respect to science in its relation to Christian commitment.

4/ *Foundationalism*

*The classic theory of theorizing in the Western world
is foundationalism.* Simply put, the goal of scientific
endeavor, according to the foundationalist, is to
form a body of theories from which all prejudice,
bias, and unjustified conjecture have been eliminated. To attain this, we must begin with a firm
foundation of certitude and build the house of theory
on it by methods of whose reliability we are equally
certain.

Austere and elegant, this theory has proved en-
dlessly attractive to Western man. It is worth stating
it a bit more precisely. The basic question the foundationalist addresses is, Under what circumstances
are we warranted in accepting a theory, and under
what circumstances in not accepting a theory? The
heart of his proposal is thus a rule for warranted
theory acceptance and nonacceptance. We can state
that rule in this way:

> **A person is warranted in accepting a theory at a
> certain time if and only if he is then warranted in
> believing that that theory belongs to genuine
> science (*scientia*).**[8]

To understand this proposed rule we must understand what is meant by saying that a theory belongs to genuine science. On this the thought of the foundationalist goes along the following lines:

> A theory *belongs to genuine science* if and only if it is justified by some foundational proposition and some human being could know with certitude that it is thus justified.[9]

And in turn,

> A proposition is *foundational* if and only if it is true and some human being could know noninferentially and with certitude that it is true.[10]

A diagram illustrating this view of the "logic" of genuine science will perhaps be helpful.

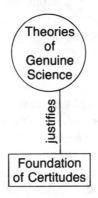

In sum, the foundationalist sees the house of genuine science as firmly based on a foundation of certitudes which can be known noninferentially. He urges that we accept or reject a given theory wholly on the basis of our warranted belief that the theory belongs or does not belong to genuine science. Only if we thus govern our acceptance of theories can we move towards eliminating prejudice, bias, and unjustified conjecture from the enterprise of theorizing.

Foundationalism has been the reigning theory of theories in the West since the high Middle Ages. It can be traced back as far as Aristotle, and since the Middle Ages vast amounts of philosophical thought have been devoted to elaborating and defending it. It has been the dominant tradition among Christians as well as among non-Christians. It has been presupposed in attacks on Christianity and on the possibility of Christian scholarship, and in defenses of Christianity and of the possibility of Christian scholarship. Aquinas, Descartes, Leibniz, Berkeley, the logical positivists—all of them and many more have been foundationalists.

Aquinas offers one classic version of foundationalism. There is, he said, a body of propositions which can be known by the natural light of reason—that is, propositions which can become self-evident to us in our present earthly state. Properly conducted scientific inquiry consists in arriving at other propositions by way of reliable inference (demonstration) from these. In addition, there are propositions that God reveals to us and which we ought to accept. A few of these (for example, that God exists) can be inferred from propositions knowable by the natural light of reason. But most of them are not of this sort. Nor can they become self-evident to us. In short, they cannot be known,[11] and we must simply believe them on the ground of the credibility of the revealer. So though faith adds to our apprehension of truth it adds only to our *believing* apprehension, not to our *knowing* apprehension. For weighing theories in the sciences, propositions that can only be believed, not *known,* have no bearing, no relevance. Aquinas' view can thus be called a *complementarist* view. Faith complements reason.

Unbelief, says Aquinas, characteristically has a profound effect on what a human being does in fact come to know, for it will tend to make him lazy, hasty, indifferent to truth. However, what *can* be known by someone who has faith can also in principle be known by someone in unbelief. A man of faith and a man of unbelief will perforce *believe* different things, and in all likelihood they will *know* different things. But the latter is not necessarily the case, for the unbeliever need not be lazy, hasty, and indifferent. Unbelief is an obstacle to knowing what can be known by a human being in his earthly state, but not an insuperable one.

A second classic view of the relation of faith and reason can be called the *preconditionalist* view. Faith is seen as a condition for arriving at a fully comprehensive, coherent, consistent, and true body of theories in the sciences. This view is implicit in Augustine's *"credo ut intelligam,"* "I believe in order that I might understand"; and I think it was the view of John Calvin.[12]

Preconditionalism need not be developed along

foundationalist lines, but if it is the suggestion might well be as follows. Lack of faith prevents one from apprehending with certitude propositions which otherwise could be thus apprehended; indeed, it even prevents one from warrantably believing that those propositions can be apprehended in that way. Note that a preconditionalist who thinks along these lines need not hold that there is some set of propositions *none* of which can be apprehended with certitude by anybody who lacks faith. He might allow that what is blocked off from apprehension varies from unbeliever to unbeliever depending on the particular quality of the unbelief.

The great challenge to the development of pre-conditionalism along these foundationalist lines is to explain *why* unbelief has this effect on one's theoretical work. Why should it be, as Anselm says (in Chapter I of the *Proslogium*), that "the smoke of our wrongdoing" prevents us from knowing what otherwise we could know, and even prevents us from warrantably believing that it can be known? Augustine points to the phenomenon of *absolutizing* as a clue. Instead of taking God as absolute, the unbeliever absolutizes something else. He loves some creature rather than the Creator, and this prevents him from apprehending with certitude some of those propositions which otherwise he could apprehend thus. Augustine does not explain exactly how absolutizing has this effect.

There is a third way in which foundationalism has been appropriated by those who have attempted to explicate the relation of faith to reason. In Protestant thought especially the suggestion has been made that the entire doctrinal content of the faith is to be found among the body of foundational certitudes. For it is held that this just consists of what the Bible teaches; and the Bible is infallible. This might be called an *incorporationist* view, for the content of the faith is incorporated within the foundation.

It is evident that each of these positions—the complementarist, the (foundational) preconditionalist, the incorporationist—bristles with ideas to be developed and problems to be dealt with. But each assumes the truth of foundationalism. And within the community of those working in philosophy of knowledge and philosophy of science foundationalism has suffered a series of deadly blows in the last 25 years. To many of those acquainted with the history of this development it now looks all but dead. So it looks to me.

Of course, it is always possible that by a feat of prodigious imagination foundationalism can be revitalized. I consider that highly improbable, and so I am persuaded that we must henceforth construct nonfoundationalist theories of theorizing. In Sections 5 and 6 I shall describe briefly the main difficulties of foundationalism, for unless we see clearly not only *that* foundationalism is collapsing but *why* it is collapsing we shall not escape the pattern it imposes וקןon our thought.

The demise of foundationalism is obviously important for the construction of a theory of theorizing acceptable to Christians. Less obviously, the demise of foundationalism is important for the cause of Christian scholarship in general. It is one thing to treat a theory of theorizing as something merely descriptive of theorizing, whose acceptance or rejection therefore is quite independent of one's other theoretical work. But foundationalism consists of a thesis as to how theorizing *should be* practiced. Foundationalism is a *normative* theory. And though I shall argue that no one who has professed to be a foundationalist has ever followed the norm to which he subscribes, yet overall the acceptance of foundationalism by Western scholars has profoundly affected their theorizing. In the case of those scholars who were Christians, its acceptance has repeatedly served to confuse and intimidate them in their theorizing. Only if the sting of foundationalism is plucked will the infection subside.

5/ Difficulties in explaining what constitutes justification of theory by foundation

As we saw, the main doctrine of the foundationalist is the normative rule that a person is warranted in accepting a theory at a certain time if and only if he is then warranted in believing that that theory belongs to genuine science. In propounding this criterion of theory acceptance the foundationalist uses two main concepts—the concept of *a theory's belonging to genuine science* and the concept of *being warranted in believing so-and-so*.

All of us grasp the concept of being warranted in believing so-and-so. This is not a concept that the foundationalist must somehow explain to us before we can understand his thesis, nor would we be justified in demanding of him an explication of the concept.

But would we be justified in requiring of the foundationalist a *general criterion* for determining when one is and when one is not warranted in believing so-and-so? I think not. In the first place, one can be warranted (and know that one is warranted) in believing so-and-so without having a satisfactory general criterion for warranted belief. I am surely warranted in my belief that I cannot jump to the moon. Yet I have no general criterion for warranted belief. So if everything else about the foundationalist's criterion is satisfactory we can accept and use it even though he gives us no general criterion for warranted belief.

Secondly, anyone who has a criterion for warranted theory-acceptance will have to use the concept of warranted belief. If anyone who makes use of this concept also has a satisfactory criterion for warranted belief, the foundationalist can simply make that criterion his. On the other hand, if no one has a satisfactory criterion for warranted belief the foundationalist is no worse off than anyone else.[13]

In short, we would not be justified in demanding of the foundationalist either a satisfactory explication of the *concept* of being warranted in believing so-and-so, or a satisfactory *criterion* as to when one is warranted in believing so-and-so. But the same cannot be said for the concept of *a theory's belonging to genuine science*. This concept does need explication, and the foundationalist offers it. Let us look at what he says; and, having discovered (if we can) what he means, let us ask whether his criterion is plausible: that we are warranted in accepting some theory if and only if we are warranted in believing that it belongs to genuine science.

The foundationalist's explication of a theory's belonging to genuine science uses two main concepts: that of a theory's being *justified* by some foundational propositions, and that of *knowing something with noninferential certitude*. In looking at each of these in turn, we shall be considering what is often called the logic of science.

We may give the name 'justification' to the relation a theory bears to the foundation if it belongs to genuine science. Exactly what sort of relation is this?

The classical view was that the relation is that of *deduction*. A theory belongs to genuine science just in case it is deducible from the foundation. One can see how this view is attractive. Deduction always and necessarily transmits truth from premises to conclusions. If we start from premises of whose truth we are certain and proceed deductively, we shall always arrive at conclusions of which we can also be certain. Obviously this nicely fits the foundationalist vision of making science a matter of firm knowledge, with bias and conjecture eliminated. Rudolf Carnap, describing in 1963 the views he had held in 1929 said that it was then his belief that "there was a certain rock bottom of knowledge . . . which was indubitable. Every other kind of knowledge was supposed to be firmly supported by this basis and likewise decidable with certainty."[14]

Today, deductivism has all but totally collapsed. The reason is simple. Many theories which seem warranted of acceptance are not deducible from any foundation. This is the case even if we assume (which is highly questionable as we shall shortly see) that the foundation contains singular propositions about observable physical objects. One difficulty that arises is that most universal propositions about physical objects would not be warranted. Take, for instance, 'All swans have wings.' The most promising candidates for foundational propositions from which this can be deduced are singular instances—propositions like '*This* swan has wings.' But even if I somehow gain the certitude that swan *a* has wings, that swan *b* has wings, and so on, it will not *deductively* follow from what I know, no matter how many such items of certitude I acquire, that *all* swans have wings. To arrive at that conclusion I would have to add the premiss 'The swans I have cited are all the swans there are.' But how could I come by a certain knowledge of *that* proposition? The conclusion seems inescapable: even so elementary a "theory" as 'All swans have wings' cannot be deductively derived from foundational propositions. Yet are we not warranted in accepting it—or, if not this one, at least some other such universal propositions?

Once deductivism was seen to be untenable, an alternative arose. We may call it *probabilism*. On this view a theory belongs to genuine science just in case it is *probable* with respect to the foundation. Obvious as this alternative may now seem to us, we should not play down the importance of the shift from deductivism to probabilism. Most of the traditional foundationalists would have refused to regard conjectures—no matter how probable—as knowledge at all. The move from deductivism to probabilism was a radical lowering of standards as to what constitutes genuine *scientia*.

But probabilism proved to have its own debilitating difficulties. Its lowered profile did not secure for it imperviousness to attack. Let us briefly see why. The point of requiring of a theory merely that it be probable with respect to the foundation if it is to belong to genuine science is that this permits inductive as well as deductive arguments from the foundational certitudes. An inductive argument will always have this structure:

> The relative frequency of observed B's among observed A's is m/n.
> Therefore, it is probable that the relative frequency of B's among all A's is m/n.

For example,

> Side 4 was observed to come up in 1/6 of the tosses of this die.
> Therefore, it is probable that side 4 will come up in 1/6 of all the tosses of this die.

A fundamental question about all such arguments is, What justifies us in drawing a conclusion of that sort from a premiss of that sort? One might reply that such arguments need no justification, that we can apprehend them noninferentially and with certitude as satisfactory. The problem with that response is that it does not seem to be true. Already in the 18th century David Hume noticed that if nature is not uniform between what we have observed (the evidence) and what we have not, then this is surely not a satisfactory mode of argument; whereas if it is thus uniform, it is satisfactory.

So the question becomes, Are we warranted in believing that nature is thus uniform? Here there are two options open to the foundationalist. He can say that we know with certitude, whether inferentially or noninferentially, that nature is uniform. But surely we do not. None of us knows, let alone knows with certitude, that those segments of the world which have been observed are uniform with those which have not been. The other option is to say that on the basis of the evidence it is *probably* true that nature is thus uniform. But that would be to offer an inductive argument—an inductive argument to justify the very principle we need to justify an inductive argument. In short, we are still in the situation that David Hume was in. We lack a justification for induction.

It is important to see that, as far as foundationalism is concerned, all probabilistic inductive arguments are equally untenable, for they all use a rule of inference that is neither known with certitude to be satisfactory nor known to be probably satisfactory. But this leaves us without any acceptable explanation of the relation theories bear to the foundation just in case they belong to genuine science. First it was demanded that a theory be provable with respect to the foundation. It turned out that most acceptable theories were not. Then it was required that a theory be probable with respect to the foundation. It turned out that none were.

Now there is nowhere in these developments a *refutation* of foundationalism. We have not proved that a foundationalist justification of induction will *never* be discovered and developed, or that no satisfactory alternative to deductivism and probabilism will ever be proposed. But the developments we have sketched have made foundationalism look like an extremely unpromising theory.

This is not the end of the story. Not all who have given up on foundationalism have dispensed with an appeal to foundations. On the contrary, an influential theory of theorizing for the empirical sciences has been proposed which in some of its versions makes an appeal to foundations. This theory has been called *falsificationism*.

Those who adopt this theory admit that the collapse of deductivism and probabilism deprives us of necessary and sufficient conditions of a foundationalist sort for a theory's belonging to genuine science. But, they insist, we can still give a *necessary* condition of a foundationalist sort for a theory's belonging to genuine science. Or, to put it the other way around, we can give a *sufficient* condition for a theory's *not* belonging to genuine science. If a theory *contradicts* the foundation it cannot belong to genuine science. So this principle is proposed:

> A theory does not belong to genuine science if it is inconsistent with the foundation and someone could know with certitude that it is inconsistent.[15]

If we have only a sufficient condition for a theory's *not* belonging to genuine science we cannot, of course, offer a *criterion* (a necessary and sufficient condition) for warranted theory acceptance. We can, though, offer a necessary condition for such acceptance. Or, to look at this too from the other side, we can offer a *sufficient* condition for warranted theory *rejection:*

> **A person is warranted in rejecting a theory at a given time if at that time he is warranted in believing that that theory does not belong to genuine science.**

It is this rule for warranted theory rejection that has sometimes been called *falsificationism.*[16]

In defense of falsificationism as a normative rule for the empirical sciences, it is argued that in fact responsible theorists in those sciences follow this rule. They do not look for confirmations of their theories; they do not try to show that some theory is *justified*. They look instead for refutations. They deduce various consequences of the theories. Then they test those consequences. If the result of their tests is that the consequences do not accord with what is known to be true, then the theory is rejected. "Once and for all," says Herman Weyl, "I wish to record my unbounded admiration for the work of the experimenter in his struggle to wrest *interpretable facts* from an unyielding Nature who knows so well how to meet our theories with a decisive *No*—or with an inaudible *Yes.*[17]

But falsificationism is not without its difficulties either. The chief of these is that it seldom instructs us to reject a theory. For seldom are theories shown to be inconsistent with what is taken as foundation. Let us see why. Suppose that you have tentatively adopted a certain theory and are now conducting a research program suggested by it. In the course of this research you come across an anomaly—some phenomenon that you did not at all expect. Suppose further that you take the existence of this phenomenon as something definitely known. Does the falsification test now instruct you forthwith to surrender the theory? Not at all. For no theory ever stands alone. Every theorist confronts the world with a whole web of theoretical and non-theoretical beliefs. And seldom will there be a direct contradiction between his theory and what he takes as indisputably known. Rather, there will at best be a contradiction between *the whole web* of his beliefs and what he takes as indisputably known. It is then up to him to decide which of his beliefs to surrender. The wisest course may be to surrender the theory under consideration. Or it may be to surrender some other theory. But for answering that question the falsification rule gives us no guidance whatsoever.[18]

Let us go back to the case of the Congregation of the Inquisition. Their reading of Holy Scripture led them to believe in the geocentric theory of the motion of heavenly bodies. Suppose that they came across some fact which was an anomaly for this theory. Should they then have concluded that the Holy Scriptures taught falsehood? Well, a host of other options were certainly available. They could, for one thing, have stuck to the geocentric theory and surrendered some other ancillary natural-scientific hypotheses. They could have concluded that the text of Holy

Scripture which they were using was corrupt at the crucial junctures. They could have concluded that though the writers of Holy Scripture *believed* that the sun traveled around the earth, they never meant to *teach* this.[19] They could have concluded that the writers of Holy Scripture were not saying that the sun *did* travel around the earth but that it *looked* that way. They could have concluded that Holy Scriptures are to be taken as authoritative only on "religious" and not on "secular" matters.[20] For deciding among these options—and others—the rule of falsification is simply irrelevant.

Or consider this illuminating little tale told by Imre Lakatos:

> The story is about an imaginary case of planetary misbehavior. A physicist of the pre-Einsteinian era takes Newton's mechanics and his law of gravitation (N), the accepted initial conditions, I, and calculates, with their help, the path of a newly discovered small planet, p. But the planet deviates from the calculated path. Does our Newtonian physicist consider that the deviation was forbidden by Newton's theory and therefore that, once established, it refutes the theory N? No. He suggests that there must be a hitherto unknown planet p' which perturbs the path of p. He calculates the mass, orbit, etc., of this hypothetical planet and then asks an experimental astronomer to test his hypothesis. The planet p' is so small that even the biggest available telescopes cannot possibly observe it: the experimental astronomer applies for a research grant to build yet a bigger one. In three years' time the new telescope is ready. Were the unknown planet p' to

be discovered, it would be hailed as a new victory of Newtonian science. But it is not. Does our scientist abandon Newton's theory and his idea of the perturbing planet? No. He suggests that a cloud of cosmic dust hides the planet from us. He calculates the location and properties of this cloud and asks for a research grant to send up a satellite to test his calculations. Were the satellite's instruments (possibly new ones, based on a little-tested theory) to record the existence of the conjectural cloud, the result would be hailed as an outstanding victory for Newtonian science. But the cloud is not found. Does our scientist abandon Newton's theory, together with the idea of the perturbing planet and the idea of the cloud which hides it? No. He suggests that there is some magnetic field in that region of the universe which disturbed the instruments of the satellite. A new satellite is sent up. Were the magnetic field to be found, Newtonians would celebrate a sensational victory. But it is not. Is this regarded as a refutation of Newtonian science? No. Either yet another ingenious auxiliary hypothesis is proposed or . . . the whole story is buried in the dusty volumes of periodicals and the story never mentioned again.[21]

The conclusion is this: even if there is a set of foundational propositions, no one has yet succeeded in stating what relation the theories that we are warranted in accepting or rejecting bear to the members of that set. Even if there is a set of foundational propositions, we are without a general logic of the sciences, and hence without a general rule for warranted theory acceptance and rejection.

6/ Difficulties in finding enough propositions to belong to the foundation

*Essential to the foundationalist's vision is the ex-*istence of a body of foundational propositions—that is, propositions which are not only true but can be know noninferentially and with certitude to be true. Do we have any good reason to think that there are any such propositions? Or, more relevantly, do we have any good reason to think that there are enough such propositions to serve as the basis for all theory acceptance and theory rejection?

Unfortunately, this latter question, which is directly relevant, does not pose a clear and definite issue. The conclusion of our preceding discussion was that the foundationalist does not have a satisfactory criterion for a theory's being *justified* by some foundational proposition. That means we do not *know* what it is for propositions to serve as a basis for theory acceptance and rejection. Consequently, to ask whether propositions knowable noninferentially and with certitude constitute an expansive enough basis for such actions is not to ask a definite question.

However, for the purposes of that earlier argument we simply assumed that some singular propositions about physical objects are foundational. (We went on to show that even if this assumption were true it would still not be the case that theories warranted of acceptance are limited to those deducible from, or probable with respect to, the foundation.) One thing we can do at this point is to consider whether that assumption was warranted. If not, we will have a double reason for rejecting foundationalism.

So the question is, Are there singular propositions about physical objects which we can know noninferentially and with certitude to be true? Can I, for instance, know noninferentially and with certitude that *My desk is brown?*

Obviously, our question will lack definiteness until some determination is made as to what is to be meant by "certitude." Now there are a number of distinct concepts that might justly be called concepts of certitude.[22] The fair procedure will be to take a concept of certitude according to which the foundation is as ample and expansive as possible while not including any propositions whose inclusion would violate the basic intent of the foundationalist. We would be arguing unfairly if we took the *narrowest* possible concept of certitude—the one which the smallest number of propositions satisfy—or if we took a concept so broad that propositions would turn out to be foundational whose turning out to be such would frustrate the basic intent of the foundationalist. For example, it would be unfair to use a concept of certitude according to which the foundation includes *false* propositions.

The concept of certitude which best satisfies these conditions is probably that of *indubitability*.

> A proposition known with certitude by someone at a given time is one which is indubitable for him at that time.[23]

So our question becomes, Are there singular propositions about physical objects which we can know noninferentially and indubitably?

The question must still be sharpened. What is meant by knowing something noninferentially? The view of the foundationalist is that if there is to be genuine *scientia* there must be some propositions, knowable with certitude to be true, by reference to which theories are justified. That is, in order to be a theory of genuine science a proposition must be obtainable from some certitudes by satisfactory rules of inference. Accordingly, if we are to avoid an endless regress or a circle, there must be propositions which we can know with certitude to be true without knowing that they are obtainable by satisfactory rules of inference from yet others which we know with certitude to be true. It is these propositions that are known noninferentially.[24]

Are there singular propositions about physical objects which someone can know noninferentially and indubitably to be true? For example, can I know noninferentially and indubitably that *My desk is brown?*

Most singular propositions about physical objects are such that if we are to know them at all we must know certain of such propositions by way of observation. So, the important question becomes, can we, by the use of our perceptual capacities, acquire a noninferential indubitable knowledge of singular propositions about physical objects? In pursuing the answer to this question, let us focus on indubitability rather than noninferentiality, for the requirement of noninferentiality is not an independent one but follows from the requirement that some of our beliefs be indubitable.

Well, not every human being will be able to acquire such knowledge. If the color of an object is at issue, for instance, one who is color blind will not be able to attain such knowledge. And not every use of one's perceptual capacities will do. If one is heavily under the influence of liquor or hallucinogens, the use of his perceptual capacities will not yield indubitability. Likewise, the use of one's perceptual capacities on objects under poor conditions will not yield it. On a foggy night brown desks do not always appear brown and desk-like, and objects that appear brown and desk-like are not always brown desks.

If there could never be (and we knew indubitably that there could never be) any discrepancy between how objects appear to us via our perceptual capacities and how they really are, then—assuming that our beliefs concerning how objects appear to us can be indubitable—we could gain indubitable knowledge about how they are. For under those circumstances if some object appeared to me brown and desk-like I could conclude that there was a brown desk which I was perceiving, and my belief would be indubitable.

Discrepancy between appearing and being, however, is one of the fundamental features of human existence. Having discovered the appearing/being distinction, we all gradually learn to cope with it. We learn laws to the effect that if one is a perceiver of such-and-such a sort, or in such-and-such a state, or if the object perceived is in such-and-such a situation, then in using one's perceptual capacities probably such-and-such objects will appear different from the way they are with respect to such-and-such properties. Further, we even learn certain laws specifying how such an object in such a condition will appear instead. We learn that a blue object under a red light not only will not appear blue but will appear purple.

Now one might raise the question whether our believing such laws can ever be a matter of indubitable knowledge. But let us pass over that difficulty and suppose that we know indubitably some laws of the form 'If one uses one's perceptual capacities under conditions of sort C, then objects of sort O will not appear as they are in respect of properties of sort P.' We would still be left with this unsettling question: How could we possibly acquire an indubitable knowledge of all such laws *and of the fact that we know all such laws?* How could we possibly acquire the indubitable knowledge that we know all the discrepancy-making conditions? How could we ever know indubitably that we had not missed one such law? Are not the ways of going wrong past finding out? But if I do not know indubitably that I know all the discrepancy-making conditions, then my present belief that I am perceiving a brown desk, grounded as it is on my knowledge that what I am perceiving appears to me brown and desk-like, can also not be indubitable. For may it not be that some noxious chemical of which I know nothing has entered my city's water supply, making this object *look* brown when it *is not* brown?

The screws can be turned yet tighter. Even if I knew indubitably that I knew all the discrepancy-making conditions, how could I acquire the indubitable knowledge that none of them obtains in a given case? But without such indubitable knowledge I still cannot infer from how something appears to how it is. Suppose I see something which appears to me brown and desk-like. I know all the discrepancy laws concerning the state of our perceptual apparatus, including one which states that when a perceiver is under the influence of drug α red desks appear brown rather than red. Now, if I am to know indubitably that this is a brown desk on the basis of my knowledge that I see something which appears brown and desk-like, I must know indubitably that I am not now under the influence of drug α (nor of anything else which puts my perceptual capacities in an abnormal state). There are ways of finding out whether my perceptual capacities are in an abnormal state or not, but such ways themselves involve perception. So I run through the perceptual tests. In order to have indubitable knowledge of the results of these tests, I need indubitable knowledge that in perceiving the results of the tests there is no discrepancy between appearing and being. I must know indubitably that I am not suffering from the effects of drug α, and the like. In short, if I am to come to the indubitable knowledge that my perceptual capacities are in their normal state by the use of my perceptual capacities, I must already have indubitable knowledge that my perceptual capacities are in their normal state.

One factor influencing how things appear to us is especially relevant to foundationalism. Psychologists have shown through many fascinating experiments that the way things appear to us is influenced by our beliefs and expectations. To an alarming degree things appear to us as we believe they are rather than as they are, and fail to appear to us as they are when we do not expect them thus to appear. This is confirmed in a startling way in the history of art, as Ernst Gombrich demonstrates in his great book *Art & Illusion*. Gombrich offers many examples of works of art praised in their day for fidelity to nature which seem quaint to us now in their odd but obvious inaccuracies. The conclusion Gombrich eventually draws is that to a great extent painters paint what they expect to see rather than what is there for them to see.

Only if our beliefs about the nature of what we are experiencing are already fully accurate will that which we experience appear to us as it really is. But this is obviously devastating to foundationalism. Perception does not yield a rock-firm base for our theories.[25] Rather, our theories must already be accurate if our perceptions are to be veridical. Perception is not insulated from theory. Theories cart along their own confirmations.

We can push even further. So far we have assumed that one can have the indubitable knowledge, via his perceptual capacities, that some object is appearing brown and desk-like. It turns out that on the basis of such knowledge concerning appearances, we cannot arrive at the indubitable knowledge that what appears brown and desk-like is a brown desk. But what about the initial assumption? *Can I* have the indubitable knowledge that *some object* is perceptually appearing to me brown and desk-like?

Reflect first on cases of delusion and illusion. Suppose I suffer from the delusion of seeing a brown desk. In such cases I am, as it were, *appeared to* "brownly" and "desk-likely." There is no object which is appearing brown and desk-like to me. The question whether or not that which I am perceiving is as it appears cannot even arise. But now consider any case in which I believe that *something* is appearing brown and desk-like to me. Will there not always be reasons such that if I believed them, I would be warranted in giving up this belief and retreating to the claim that I am just being appeared to brownly and desk-likely? In short, I may *believe* that *something* is appearing brown and desk-like to me. But I do not know that indubitably. In retreating to the more guarded claim that I am being appeared to brownly and desk-likely I have perhaps arrived at what we were looking for—an item of indubitable knowledge. But notice what it is—a claim about myself and my state of consciousness. Along the way we have discarded singular propositions about physical objects from the body of indubitables, and thus from the foundation.

It may be that though we cannot have *indubitable* knowledge of the truth of singular propositions about physical objects, yet we are warranted in believing some of them on the basis of foundational propositions about our states of consciousness. In fact no thinker has ever displayed any such warrant, nor is it easy to see how it could be done. From a set of propositions specifying how I have been appeared to one can, by straight probabilistic induction, infer how I will probably be appeared to in the future. But what principle will justify me in inferring, from such propositions, that probably some *object* was appearing to me? And then there is the prior difficulty that, on foundationalist grounds, inductive arguments in general are unacceptable.

In summary, it seems distinctly unlikely that the set of indubitables is ample enough to support all theorizing. Certain propositions about our states of consciousness belong to the foundation. But science deals not just with states of consciousness but with all sorts of "objective" entities—trees, minerals, motion of bodies, and the like. It seems unlikely that from our introspective knowledge of propositions about our own states of consciousness we could erect the whole structure of objective science. It seems even less likely that there is any other foundation of indubitables on which we can erect it.

It is possible to make the radical response at this point that only in such "nonempirical" disciplines as logic and mathematics do we have genuine *scientia*. For only here do we have theories derived by satisfactory rules of inference from indubitables. A full exploration of the latter claim is here well beyond our scope. Suffice it to remark that the Euclidean model, in which a mathematical system is constructed by beginning with self-evidently true propositions and proceeding by the use of self-evidently satisfactory rules, has been left far behind. The mathematician and the logician today begin with axioms that are far from self-evident. Then they proceed to construct deductions which they hope will not yield propositions that are self-evidently false. Along the way the air of implausibility—and of arbitrariness to avoid paradox—is very thick indeed.

7/ *What has not been claimed*

On all fronts foundationalism is in bad shape. It seems to me that there is nothing to do but give it up for mortally ill and learn to live in its absence. Theorizing is without a foundation of indubitables.

In saying this I do not at all mean to deny that there is an objective reality with a nature independent of what we all conceive and believe. Nothing I have said requires the affirmation that man is the creator of that which is.

Nor do I mean to deny that you and I can attain true belief concerning that objective reality. Nothing I have said requires the repudiation of truth as a legitimate and attainable goal of inquiry.

Nor do I mean to deny that you and I can attain knowledge of that objective reality. Nothing I have said requires the profession of cosmic agnosticism.

Nor do I mean to deny that we are warranted in accepting some from among the thicket of human beliefs and in rejecting others. Nothing I have said requires the profession of ''anything goes.''

I mean just to affirm that the proposed rule for warranted theory acceptance is untenable. It is not the case that one is warranted in accepting some theory if and only if one is warranted in believing that it is justified by propositions knowable noninferentially and with certitude. From this it does not follow that there is no structured reality independent of our conceivings and believings—though the difficulties of foundationalism have led many to this position. Nor does it follow that we must give up truth as the goal of theoretical inquiry—though the difficulties of foundationalism have made this view particularly attractive to many. Nor does it follow that we can never know the truth—though the difficulties of foundationalism have led to a wave of agnosticism. Nor does it follow that one belief is as warranted for me as another. All that follows is that theorizing is without a foundation of indubitables.

Our future theories of theorizing will have to be nonfoundationalist ones.

8/ Will the Bible save foundationalism?

Unsettling as it may be for many Christians, it must be firmly said that in the sense of "foundation" explained, the Bible also does not provide us with a foundation for theorizing. Reading and interpreting the Bible is not a procedure for arriving at propositions knowable noninferentially and indubitably to be true.

Christians holding a foundationalist view of science have often been tempted to believe that the Bible does provide such a foundation. The Bible, they say, contains the propositions God reveals, and God cannot err. Some have gone so far as to say that this stock of indubitables is sufficient *by itself* for the construction of scientific theory. Most, however, have allowed that only if biblically obtained indubitables are supplemented with those obtained by reflection and those obtained by observation would we have a foundation adequate to weigh all theories. I think that much of the motivation behind the formulation of traditional theories of biblical infallibility has been the holding of this sort of view. It has been assumed that science—and human knowledge generally—must have a foundation of certitude. What better source for such certitude for the Christian than the Bible, or the Bible along with reflection and experience?

Thoroughly considering this matter would involve probing the understanding of Scripture and revelation presupposed,[26] an effort that would take us much too far afield. For our purposes it is enough to show that even if this view of Scripture were correct the Bible could not provide us with a foundation for theorizing.

Suppose that the Bible is in fact infallible in the strongest sense: that all the propositions asserted in it and all the propositions they presuppose are true. Suppose that this is so because all these propositions are revealed by God, who cannot err. Obviously, Scripture by itself would not yet be an adequate foundation for theorizing under these conditions. To take one example, neither Bohr's theory of the atom nor its denial can be derived from the Scriptures.

But let us set this difficulty off to the side. Suppose it is true that Scripture contains only what God reveals, and that God cannot err. Can we, by reading and interpreting Scripture, arrive at an indubitable knowledge of the propositions it contains?

The difficulties with saying Yes to this question are all familiar ones.[27] To begin, notice that it is a double claim that is being made: (1) God who cannot err, reveals propositions; and (2) Scripture contains those propositions God reveals and *only* those he reveals. But how could we know indubitably that even the latter of these was true, let alone the former?

May it not be that all our copies of the Scriptures have been corrupted somewhere along the way? Is it not clear from the history of textual transmission that I do not know indubitably that my copy contains only what God reveals? Notice that it does the foundationalist no good to fall back on the argument that the original or autograph of the Scripture contained exactly what God revealed, for that autograph is no longer available.

Nevertheless, let us go a step further and suppose that the transmission has been fully accurate, and that it is somehow possible for us to acquire the indubitable knowledge that it has been. It will still be necessary for the foundationalist to attain the indubitable knowledge that what stood in that original is exactly what God revealed. But how can he possibly acquire such knowledge? How, indeed, could the original writer have known that? On the most mechanical view of the matter the biblical writers set down words which somehow they heard. But people "hear things" all the time. How could Amos, say, have had the indubitable knowledge that what he was hearing and what he was writing was what God was saying? Perhaps, indeed, he knew. But did he know *indubitably* in the foundationalist's sense of the term? Would it have been *impossible* that he should have had a reason which would have warranted him in disbelieving? Suppose he had discovered that some clever enemies of his had deceived him by whispering things from behind the rocks while he was tending his sheep. Would that not be a reason to warrant disbelief that he was hearing what God was saying?

Some have responded that the believer knows at once—by "the testimony of the Holy Spirit"—that what the Bible says is what God revealed without going through this whole chain of determining with surety that his copy is the outcome of a correct transmission and that the original writer was really setting down what God revealed. Possibly so. Again, however, the question is: But does he know this *indubitably?* Couldn't there be a reason which would warrant him in disbelieving? Suppose persuasive evidence were presented that some of the Pastoral Epistles were written by fourth-century Egyptian priests. Wouldn't that be such a reason?

Let us go one more step. Suppose that it is somehow possible for human beings to acquire the indubitable knowledge that our copies of the Scriptures record exactly what God revealed. Is it also open to us to acquire the indubitable knowledge that we properly understand what is said in these Scriptures? How might we attain such knowledge? Does not the welter of different interpretations make it most unlikely that any such knowledge can be attained? So even if the Bible were a book of indubitables, of what benefit would it be if we cannot indubitably apprehend them?

The conclusion is inescapable. The Bible will not save foundationalism.

But that is the only conclusion from what has

been said in this section. Most emphatically it does not follow that the Christian cannot have any confidence in what he believes. Nor does it follow that none of what the Christian believes has the status of knowledge. All that follows is that our reading and interpreting of Scripture does not provide us with a body of indubitably known propositions by reference to which we can govern all our acceptance and nonacceptance of theories.

9/ The structure of theory-weighing

It is time for us to begin to analyze the nature of theorizing. At the outset, we observe that some theories specify what ought to be done. That is true, as we said at the end of Section 4, of the foundationalist theory itself. It is a thesis about how theorizing should be done. For our purposes we can put such normative theories to the side and concentrate on descriptive theories—generalizations to the effect that some or all members of a set of entities possess certain properties or stand in certain relations. The set of entities in question we shall call the *scope* of the theory. For example, if I entertain the theory that all the chairs in my office originated in Canton, Ohio, then the set of chairs in my office belongs to the *scope* of that theory—as does Canton, Ohio. To propound a descriptive theory, then, is to claim that the entities within its scope fit the generalization being made.

Some theories, particularly in the natural sciences, are predictive: so-and-so will be the case given such-and-such initial conditions. But not all theories are predictive. Nor are all theories "explanatory'' in any very natural sense of that word. All, however, specify that some pattern is present within the theory's scope.

We shall pass over the question of whether every general proposition to the effect that some or all members of a set of entities possess certain properties or stand in certain relations should be regarded as a theory. Perhaps a generalization must satisfy some further conditions if it is to be regarded as a theory. Or perhaps a generalization may be considered a theory on some occasions but not on others, depending on how it is functioning. For our purposes it will not be necessary to settle these matters, since nothing in the argument will hang on whether or not some general proposition to which I refer is a theory.

In any case I shall not assume that theories are propounded or entertained only in the pursuit of some *Wissenschaft*. The fisherman who suggests that fish will not bite after a heavy rain seems to me to be propounding a theory. In other words scientific activity is not to be differentiated from other human activities on the ground that it deals with theories, nor even on the ground that it deals with theories of a special kind—*scientific* theories. Theories first devised and accepted in the pursuit of some science often enter subsequently into the nonscientific pursuits of members of society. Conversely, theories from ordinary life have frequently been taken over by scientists. Neither is science to be differentiated because scientists perform some unique act with respect to theories. In the pursuit of science people *devise* theories; in the pursuit of nonscientific activities they do so as well. In the pursuit of science people *weigh* theories; in the pursuit of nonscientific activities they do so as well. Science and ordinary life can be viewed as on a continuum with respect to the presence of theories and with respect to the actions performed on those theories. What is eminently characteristic of science is the use of theories to suggest and guide research programs. But on reflection even this can be seen as making science different only in degree from ordinary life.[28]

It is probably true (as several recent writers have suggested) that those who work in the sciences spend relatively little of their time *weighing* theories, that is, deciding whether to accept or reject them.[29] Rather, taking various theories for granted they spend most of their time making these more precise or engaging in research problems suggested by them or determining the data which bear on them with more precision, and so forth. For our purposes, however, it will be most illuminating to begin with an analysis of the weighing of theories.

In order for me to weigh a theory with respect to whether the pattern claimed is indeed in its scope, I must have beliefs about the entities within the scope.[30] At least some of these beliefs must be such that I take them as *data*. That is to say, some must be of the type that I require the theory at the very least to be consistent with them. This is minimal. In the case of my theory that all the chairs in my office originate in Canton, Ohio, our first consideration comes to this: if I have no beliefs about my office, the chairs in it, and Canton, with which I require the Canton-origination theory to be consistent for me to accept it, I simply cannot weigh that theory with respect to what it claims. At the center of all weighing of theory with respect to the presence or absence of the pattern claimed is a *decision* to take certain of one's beliefs about the entities within the theory's scope as data for one's weighing of the theory.

We have seen that we cannot make this decision by reference to a fund of foundational certitudes. We cannot resolve to take as data only what we can know indubitably. For that would yield no data—or, to put it more cautiously, far too little. If I am to weigh a theory's claim there is no option to my taking as data that which I find myself believing to be true. Confronted as we are with the fact that we lack a shared foundation, each of us has no choice but "to one's own self be true."

Now it happens repeatedly that more than one competing theory will be consistent with all that I take as data. My decision between them must then be made on other grounds. Yet it remains true: there can be no weighing of theory with respect to what is claimed without taking as data some of one's beliefs about entities in the theory's scope.

In weighing a theory one always brings along the whole complex of one's beliefs. One does not strip away all but those beliefs functioning as data relative to the theory being weighed. On the contrary, one remains cloaked in belief—aware of some strands, unaware of most. I wish especially to single out two sorts of components from this cloak of belief.

For one thing, there will always be a large set of beliefs such that one's holding them is a condition of one's accepting as data that which one does. Let us call these *data-background beliefs*. If in weighing some theory I take as datum that this desk is brown, that may be because I believe that when I observed the desk my senses were in their proper state for discovering its color; that may be because I believe that when I observed the desk it was lit in the proper way for my discovering its color by observation; and so on. What should be noticed is that among the data-background beliefs for a given person's weighing of a given theory there will in turn be a great many theories. That which the scientist takes as data he does so because of his acceptance of an enormously complicated web of theory. However, for the weighing of a given theory at a given time all such data-background theories are taken as unproblematic. The data-background theories are, on that occasion, not subjected to weighing.

For our purposes it is even more important to bring to attention a second component in the cloak of beliefs one wears while weighing a theory. Everyone who weighs a theory has certain beliefs as to what constitutes an acceptable *sort* of theory on the matter under consideration. We can call these *control* beliefs. They include beliefs about the requisite logical or aesthetic structure of a theory, beliefs about the entities to whose existence a theory may correctly commit us, and the like. Control beliefs function in two ways. Because we hold them we are led to *reject* certain sorts of theories—some because they are inconsistent with those beliefs; others because, though consistent with our control beliefs, they do not comport well with those beliefs. On the other hand control beliefs also lead us to *devise* theories. We want theories that are consistent with our control beliefs. Or, to put it more stringently, we want theories that comport as well as possible with those beliefs.[31]

It was one of Ernst Mach's control beliefs that theories postulating nonsensory entities are unsatisfactory. Any theory that postulated a nonsensory entity he rejected as not even a satisfactory candidate for acceptance. But also, in accord with this control belief he himself set about to reconstruct physics on a sensationalistic basis. In short, control beliefs function both negatively and positively in the propounding and weighing of theories.

At the very beginning of our discussion I cited several other examples of control beliefs. The concept is so central in what follows that it will perhaps be worth citing another instance: one that has been much discussed in recent years. Near the beginning of *Beyond Freedom and Dignity* B. F. Skinner presents his requirements for acceptable sorts of psychological theories. Very forthrightly he says:

> The task of a scientific analysis is to explain how the behavior of a person as a physical system is

related to the conditions under which the human species evolved and the conditions under which the individual lives. . . .

We can follow the path taken by physics and biology by turning directly to the relation between behavior and the environment and neglecting supposed mediating states of mind. Physics did not advance by looking more closely at the jubilance of a falling body, or biology by looking at the nature of vital spirits, and we do not need to try to discover what personalities, states of mind, feelings, traits of character, plans, purposes, intentions, or the other perquisites of autonomous man really are in order to get on with a scientific analysis of behavior.[32]

Beginning with some person's weighing of a theory we have made, within his beliefs, a threefold distinction between *data beliefs, data-background beliefs,* and *control beliefs.* It should be emphasized that this is not a distinction as to the *essence* of beliefs but rather a distinction as to how beliefs *function*— how they function relative to a given person's weighing of a given theory on a given occasion. What functions as a data-background belief, or as a control belief, in a given person's weighing of a given theory on one occasion may on another occasion be the theory under consideration. On a given occasion Newton's laws of motion may be the theory which is being weighed and certain beliefs about the optical features of telescopes may remain as background to the data. On another occasion—perhaps because of the observation of some anomaly within astronomy

—the Newtonian theory may be moved into the background as unproblematic and various assumptions about the optics of the telescope may be moved into the foreground for weighing and testing. What also happens sometimes is that a belief which on a given occasion functions as a data belief against which a theory is weighed is on another occasion itself weighed by taking the theory as unproblematic.

My contention in what follows is that the religious beliefs of the Christian scholar ought to function as *control* beliefs within his devising and weighing of theories. This is not the only way they ought to function. For example, they also ought to help shape his views on what it is important to have theories about. Nor does that exhaust their function. But their functioning as control beliefs is absolutely central to the work of the Christian scholar. It is this function that I shall concentrate on.

10/ *Authentic Christian commitment*

To carry the discussion further, we should look more closely at the expression "authentic Christian commitment," which will figure heavily in what follows. Let us see, at least in skeletal fashion, what is the content of such commitment. In order to do so, I shall begin with a characterization of *actual,* rather than authentic, commitment.

To be a Christian is to be fundamentally committed to being a Christ-follower. From the very beginning that has differentiated Christians from others. To be a Christian is also, of course, to belong to a certain community—a community with a tradition. But what identifies this community is that its members are those who are fundamentally committed to being Christ-followers.

It is crucial to the character of this community with a tradition that it has certain sacred writings, those of the Old and New Testaments. These Scriptures are on the one hand expressions of the religion of ancient persons and peoples. But they have also been judged by the community of Christ-followers at large to be authoritative guides for the thought and life of those who would be Christ-followers.[33]

Anyone who is fundamentally committed to being a Christ-follower will in consequence do and believe certain things. One cannot have that fundamental commitment without its being realized in some specific and definite complex of action and belief. We can, when referring to a specific person, call the complex of action and belief in which his fundamental commitment is *in fact* realized his *actual* Christian commitment.[34]

But committing yourself to be a Christ-follower also presupposes that you have some conviction about the complex of action and belief that your following of Christ *ought* to be realized in. On the matter of what that is, Christians of course disagree widely (as they do on the issue of how one ought to go about finding out). Yet every Christian, whether liberal or conservative, has some notion of how his fundamental commitment ought to be realized. And the complex of action and belief that its realization *ought* in fact to assume, for any given person, is what I shall call his *authentic* Christian commitment.

It is important for what follows that I briefly describe the shape of what in my judgment constitutes our authentic assent. From times most ancient man has departed from the pattern of responsibilities God awarded him at creation. A multitude of evils has followed. But God was not content to leave man in the mire of his misery. In response to man's sin and its resultant evils he resolved to bring about renewal. Indeed, he has already been acting on that resolve, centrally and decisively in the life, death, and resurrection of Jesus Christ, but more generally by calling out a people who will make decisively ultimate in their lives the challenge to be witnesses, agents, and evidences of his work of renewal. *Witnesses*—in that this people is called to proclaim that God is working in the world to bring about an order of things in accord with the goals he had when he created them. *Agents*—in that this people is called to do what it can to bring about such an order. And *evidences*—in that this people is called to give indication in its life of what such an order would be like. One's following of Christ, then, ought to be actualized by taking up in decisively ultimate fashion God's call to share in the task of being witness, agent, and evidence of the coming of his kingdom.

In thus sharing in the work of being witness, agent, and evidence of God's work of renewal the members of God's people would constitute themselves a band of disciples of Jesus Christ. For it was he who was the principal witness, the decisive agent, the one who gave the most lucid evidence.

This (expressed as briefly as possible) is how in my judgment our following of Christ *ought* to be actualized. Notice that on this view authentic Christian commitment is not to be identified with subscription to dogmas. Indeed, it is not to be identified with the believing of propositions, dogmatic or otherwise.[35] But notice also that it does *incorporate* this in several ways.

The people in whose work one would share is

called to proclaim certain things, to make certain pronouncements, to tell forth what is taking place in history. And of course it is presupposed that they believe those things. That is one way belief is incorporated within Christian commitment. There is a second way. The people is called to give evidence of the new life. That involves treating nature with delight and respect and acting in solidarity with the socially oppressed. But equally it involves *believing* certain things—among others, those things taught in the creeds. Thus though authentic Christian commitment is not to be identified with believing certain things, it does in fact have a belief-content.[36]

For the purposes of what follows it is important to recognize that the propositions included within the belief-content of our authentic Christian commitment are not just about "the supernatural." They are as much about this world and its inhabitants as they are about God. If that is not already evident it would be fully so if we elaborated *what* it is that God calls us to say and do and be.[37]

Authentic Christian commitment, as I have explained it, is relative to persons and to times. For authentic Christian commitment is how one's Christ-following *ought* to be actualized. And that varies not only from person to person but also from time to time within a given person's life. What I ought to be doing today by way of following Christ differs from what you ought to be doing, and from what I ought to have been doing when I was younger. Likewise what I am obliged to believe as a follower of Christ differs from what someone else is obliged to believe, and differs from what I as a child was obliged to believe. So authentic Christian commitment as a whole, but also the belief-content thereof, is relative to persons and times. One might insist that there are certain propositions which belong to the belief-content of all authentic Christian commitment whatever. Probably so. But certainly they will be few and simple.[38]

11/ *How authentic commitment ought to function in theorizing*

I said at the end of Section 9 that the religious beliefs of the Christian scholar ought to function as control beliefs within his devising and weighing of theories. I can now put that point more accurately. The Christian scholar ought to allow the belief-content of his authentic Christian commitment to function as control within his devising and weighing of theories.[39] For he like everyone else ought to seek consistency, wholeness, and integrity in the body of his beliefs and commitments. Since his fundamental commitment to following Christ ought to be decisively ultimate in his life, the rest of his life ought to be brought into harmony with it. As control, the belief-content of his authentic commitment ought to function both negatively and positively. Negatively, the Christian scholar ought to reject certain theories on the ground that they conflict or do not comport well with the belief-content of his authentic commitment.[40] And positively he ought to devise theories which comport as well as possible with, or are at least consistent with, the belief-content of his authentic commitment.

The belief-content of our authentic commitment incorporates, for example, the belief that one of the fundamental things that makes human beings unique among earthlings lies in the fact that they and they alone have been ''graced'' by God with responsibilities. That in turn presupposes that man was created in such a way as to be free to carry out or not to carry out those responsibilities. For Christian scholars these propositions, accordingly, ought to function as *control* over the sorts of theories which we are willing to accept. Now as far as I can tell, many behaviorists and Freudians either deny human freedom and responsibility entirely, or deny them at points where the Christian would affirm their presence. If so, we ought to reject such theories. But we ought also to go on and develop theories in psychology which do comport with, or are consistent with, the belief-content of our authentic commitment. Only when the belief-content of the Christian scholar's authentic Christian commitment enters into his or her devising and weighing of psychological theories in this way can it be said that he or she is fully serious both as scholar and as Christian.

We should highlight several corollaries of this way of seeing the matter.

(1) The belief-content of the Christian scholar's authentic commitment will not, by and large, actually contain his theories. The theories are not already there in the belief-content, just waiting to be extracted. Perhaps that is the case because the requisite general propositions are not, as part of the belief-

content, *theories*. On that I have no opinion one way or the other. In any case it is true because the requisite general propositions are not there at all. The same holds when we consider the belief-content of the scholar's *actual* commitment. The version of Christian commitment exhibited by the Congregation of the Inquisition in the seventeenth century incorporated the geocentric theory of the motion of the heavenly bodies. But even it included neither more specific theories about the paths of specific heavenly bodies, nor a more general theory of motion (mechanics). Now it sometimes happens that the belief-content of a scholar's actual commitment *suggests* a theory to him. But often not even that is the case. For the most part a Christian scholar has to obtain his theories by using the same capacities of imagination that scholars in general use.

Connected with this is the fact that the Bible cannot function as a black book of theories for the Christian scholar. That man is a free and responsible being is indeed a philosophical theory, and perhaps also a high-level psychological theory; and it is something contained within the biblical teaching. But the *detailed* psychological theories which fall under this high-level psychological or philosophical theory are not to be found in the Bible.

(2) With respect to many matters, especially matters of detail, there are more than one theory which will satisfy the belief-content of a scholar's authentic Christian commitment. Two alternative theories of musical harmony, for instance, or two

alternative theories of mathematical sets, may each be consistent with a scholar's authentic commitment —even comport well with it. One often hears it said that Christians, by virtue of their common commitment, *ought* to share all their scientific theories in common. Part of the reason why this is not in fact the case is that people's actual commitment falls short of their authentic commitment; part of the reason is that authentic commitment differs from person to person. But furthermore, even one person's *authentic* commitment allows scope for alternative theories. The presence of some theoretical dispute among Christian scholars is not, by itself, sufficient as proof of deficiency in the character of the commitment of one or more of them.

(3) The belief-content of a scholar's *actual* Christian commitment is not, by and large, the source of the data for his theory weighing, and the belief-content of his *authentic* commitment could not, by and large, be the source thereof. For example, the data which some person has for his weighing of a theory of poetic metaphor will consist of beliefs concerning some of the world's poetic metaphors. If he has acted as a responsible scholar he will have acquired most of these data by taking careful note of the poetic metaphors that came his way. He will not have derived them simply by extracting them from the belief-content of his actual commitment; and he could not have derived them by extracting them from the belief-content of his authentic commitment, for they are not there to be extracted.

There are exceptions to this generalization. Certain data-beliefs may be extracted from the belief-content of our authentic commitment as well as by observation of the world. In some cases experience may confirm what one already believed. In other cases a body of data-beliefs relevant to the weighing of a given theory may be such that some of its members were gotten by extraction and others were gotten (and could only have been gotten) by observation. For example, some of the data-beliefs against which one weighs some theory of human aggression may be taught in the Scriptures, and on that account incorporated within one's authentic commitment; while others could only have come from one's own observation of living human beings. For certain theories it is even possible that all of one's data beliefs come solely from the belief-content of one's authentic commitment. But by and large the Christian scholar arrives at the data for his theory weighing by using the same strategies as everyone else— by observing and reflecting on the world about him.[41]

From these corollaries it is clear that it will often be insufficient for a Christian scholar to propose as his reason for holding some theory the fact that he is a Christian (i.e., that the theory is entailed by the belief-content of his authentic commitment). The belief-content of his authentic commitment will frequently neither contain nor entail theories on the matters that he as a scholar considers. Further, when functioning as control, it will normally allow for alternative theories. Thus he will have to justify his preference, if he *can* justify it, by reference to his data beliefs. But normally his data beliefs too will not be derived from the belief-content of his authentic commitment.

(4) Especially important to notice is that, on this view of the matter, one's authentic Christian commitment ought to function *internally* to scholarship, in the search for and the weighing of theories.

Christian scholars have classically attempted to relate their commitment to their theorizing in one of three ways. Sometimes they have tried to harmonize the belief-content of their actual Christian commitment with the results of theorizing by introducing revisions into their view of what constitutes authentic commitment. This is how various Christian scholars eventually came to accept the heliocentric theory of planetary motion, the evolutionary theory concerning the origin of species, the documentary hypothesis concerning the origins of the Pentateuch, and the like. Secondly, Christian scholars have tried repeatedly to set the theories and data of science within a larger Christian context. They have tried to discover some pattern into which the theories and data of some particular science along with the belief-content of what they regard as authentic commitment fit together. Thirdly, they have repeatedly proposed distinctively Christian applications of the results of scientific theorizing to the problems of human life.

Common to the three strategies of harmonizing,

setting theories within a context, and applying them is their *conformism* with respect to science. They all take for granted that science is OK as it is. In none of them is there any *internal* relation between Christian commitment and what goes on within the sciences. In none of them does Christian commitment enter into the devising and weighing of theories within the sciences.

But the person who exhibits authentic Christian commitment cannot take for granted that the data beliefs and theories of contemporary scientists are true. The most obvious reason is that contemporary scientists *as* scientists disagree. One has to choose. But even if that were not the case within some branch of contemporary science, if all the "experts" in that field agreed, why should the Christian (or anyone else) surrender all his critical faculties in the face of it? The "experts," after all, will have practiced their science with their control beliefs. There is no reason for me to assume that mine are theirs, or that a science in accord with theirs will be in accord with mine.

(5) Rare will be the Christian scholar all of whose control beliefs are contained within his actual Christian commitment. This is justifiably the case. The reasons why a medical researcher rejects the theory lying behind the Chinese practice of acupuncture as not even the sort of theory he will entertain will most likely have little if anything to do with his religion. Rather, it will have to do with his being imbued with a whole orientation to disease

developed in the Western world within the last century. In general, no one is *just* a Christian. He is also, say, an American, a Caucasian, a member of the middle class, of somewhat paranoid personality. All of these appellations suggest characteristic sets of beliefs which, in the appropriate circumstances, may function as control within his theory-devising and theory-weighing.

(6) In some cases a Christian scholar and a non-Christian scholar may each justifiably accept a particular scientific theory. For a given theory may accord with the control beliefs of the non-Christian scholar and also with the belief-content of the authentic commitment of the Christian scholar.

That there is this sort of convergence seems obvious. The point is worth making only because of the rampant notion that if some theory acceptable to a Christian is also acceptable to some non-Christian scholar, then the claim that there is such a thing as Christian scholarship is absurd. What is in fact absurd is a concept of Christian scholarship that leads to such a conclusion.

On the other hand, there may be less ''shared ground'' than one might suppose at first glance. One is inclined to think that low-level theories will especially exhibit it. But low-level theories in science often presuppose high-level theories. And it may well be, in many cases, that unnoticed features of these high-level theories, or of complex hierarchical theories, make them in fact unacceptable either to the Christian scholar or to some non-Christian scholar. It should also be noticed that a theory in accord both with the authentic commitment of some Christian scholar and with the control beliefs of some non-Christian scholar may not be in accord with the control beliefs of some other non-Christian scholar. Likewise, given that authentic commitment differs from person to person, it may not be in accord with the authentic commitment of other Christian scholars.

(7) If we were foundationalists we would insist that nothing may be used as a control on our weighing of theories unless it itself either belongs to a fund of foundational certitudes or can be justified thereby. But we have found foundationalism untenable. Accordingly any such insistence would be out of order. Neither the data against which we weigh our theories nor the controls that we lay on our weighing of theories can be derived from a foundation of certitudes.

12/ The application of this theory of theorizing to theology

Christian theology is no exception to our general theory concerning the proper relation of Christian commitment to theory-devising and theory-weighing. It does, however, offer a quite idiosyncratic illustration of it. It is especially important to keep in mind when considering theology that our threefold distinction between data beliefs, data-background beliefs, and control beliefs is a distinction as to how beliefs function relative to a given person's weighing of a given theory on a given occasion. A belief which functions one way in one such event may function a different way in another.

The dogmatic theologian devises theories concerning God and his relation to us and the world (or, on the view of some, concerning how we ought to *think* about God and his relation to us and the world). The word "devise" is used advisedly. As an examination of the writings of dogmatic theologians will show, the theologian does not confine himself to extracting those propositions which are his theories from the content of his actual commitment. Perhaps he arrives at some by this method, but certainly not all. Having obtained his theories he weighs them by taking as data, among other beliefs of his, those which belong to the belief-content of what he regards as his authentic Christian commitment. For this, of course, includes beliefs concerning God and his relation to us and the world. Lastly, the belief-content of the theologian's authentic commitment ought all the while to be functioning also as control over his theory-devising and theory-weighing.

The dogmatic theologian customarily does something else as well. He tries to determine what constitutes authentic Christian commitment for himself and others. It is true, as I suggested earlier, that every Christian has *some* view on what constitutes authentic commitment for himself. So what is characteristic of the theologian is not that he has views on this matter, but that he develops them with care and thoroughness. This action of determining what constitutes authentic Christian commitment is different in principle from that of devising and weighing theories concerning God and his relation to us and the world (and also from that of devising and weighing theories as to how we ought to *think* about God and his relation to us and the world). It is one thing to contend that such-and-such is true concerning God and his relation to us and the world, quite another to contend that believing such-and-such is essential to authentic Christ-following. Few if any theologians would deny that one need not believe everything in their books in order to exhibit authentic commitment. Yet these two activities of the theologian are intimately related, by virtue of the fact that everyone's authentic commitment incorporates views concerning God and his relation to us and the world—the very topic that the theologian discusses.

Repeatedly, an effect of the double activity of the theologian has been that a proposition first formulated by someone in the course of his theological activities has subsequently come to be regarded, by himself and others, as part of the belief-content of their authentic Christian commitment. The theory of biblical infallibility was thus promoted in Protestantism; similarly the theory of transubstantiation in Catholicism; and various dispensationalist theories in sectarian Protestantism. General theories concerning the development of dogma have been proposed to deal with the basic structure of these shifts in what is regarded as authentic commitment. [42]

I need not stress the peculiar dangers in this. Simply stated, theologians may lead people astray. To cope with this hazard some have tried to formulate a general distinction between the theories of the theologian and the belief-content of authentic Christian commitment, urging that no seepage be allowed from the former into the latter. [43] People have attempted to distinguish, for example, between the activity of dogmatic theorizing and the activity of faith confession, suggesting that the church in its teaching and preaching activities confine itself to the latter. [44] Now no doubt there is some distinction to be made out between these two activities. But from the fact that the distinction can be made out it does not follow that no part of the content of faith confession and dogmatic theorizing is shared. It does not follow that a proposition formulated by the theologian in the course of theological activity may not also appear in someone's confession of faith. Even if we self-consciously respect the general distinction between theologizing and confessing, the desired absence of seepage is not assured. Indeed, I see no general strategy for obtaining it. It is all too natural that a proposition first formulated by some theologian should subsequently be regarded as part of the belief-content of his or other people's authentic commitment. Nor is it clear to me that this development ought invariably to be prevented. Is it not possible that some theologian in the course of his activity would be the first to formulate what is in fact part of the belief-content of his and other people's authentic Christian commitment?

The results of the work of *biblical* theologians also frequently enter into what is regarded as belonging to authentic Christian commitment. Let us see why. The biblical theologian attempts to provide an interpretation of the biblical writings. In doing so he uses principles of interpretation, of *hermeneutics*. Often his work will go beyond the use of such principles to the formulation and defense of what he regards as correct principles. Now in providing interpretation and in formulating and defending his principles of interpretation, the content of his Christian commitment will function mainly as control beliefs rather than as data beliefs. It will condition his acceptance and formation of theories. That marks his work as quite different from that of the dogmatic theologian, who, in weighing theories about God and his relation to us and the world, finds that the belief-content of what he regards as his authentic commitment contains beliefs on these very matters and so treats them as data beliefs. But what is relevant as data to the *biblical* theologian's weighing of his theories is not what he believes about God and his relation to us and the world but rather what he believes about the content of the biblical writings— not, for example, what he believes about God but rather what he believes about *what the biblical writings say* about God.

There is, of course, an important additional factor: the Christian community takes these biblical writings as properly guiding the thoughts and lives of Christ-followers. Just what it is in them that ought to guide Christians will be a matter for the *dogmatic* theologian to discuss insofar as he discusses what constitutes authentic commitment. But no matter what his conclusion, the results of the *biblical* theologian's work cannot help influencing what Christians regard as the belief-content of their authentic commitment. For example, the familiar contention of contemporary biblical theologians that the biblical view of "soul" is very different from the Platonic view has powerfully influenced the views of many people as to the belief-content of authentic commitment—precisely because a roughly Platonic view had been so widely held for so long. Yet further, not only do the biblical theologian's *interpretations* cause revisions in people's views as to the content of their authentic commitment. Sometimes the very *hermeneutical principles* of the theologian become part of what people regard as the content of their authentic commitment, with the result that proposals as to changes in such principles are viewed as proposals for departures from the true faith.

That the work of the biblical theologian has this effect is often viewed with as much alarm as the fact that the work of the dogmatic theologian can have the same consequence. Hence, the doctrine of the perspicuity of Scripture is often urged as a defense against the possibility of such revisions. But I see no way whatever to prevent them. How can the line be drawn between biblical scholarship and the careful, faithful reading of the Scriptures which ought to guide our thoughts and lives? Are we not all committed to some hermeneutical principle or other in our reading? Does not some such principle function as a control belief for each of us? And though we may be tempted to make our own such principle part of what we regard as the belief-content of our authentic commitment, should we not in fact be willing to submit it to critique? For all the dangers in particular cases, why should such developments in general be prevented? Can the scholar not in fact present us with better interpretations of the biblical writings and better principles of interpretation? Given the function of the biblical writings in the Christian community, should that capability on his part not influence our views as to what constitutes our authentic commitment?[45]

13/ The impact of theorizing on commitment

What happens when a person becomes convinced that, within the body of his belief, incompatibility has emerged—whether this incompatibility be logical contradiction or the weaker one of lack of comportment?

The actual responses in such cases are varied. But the responsible course is to seek to revise one's beliefs in a way that will make the incompatibility disappear. As we saw earlier such revision can in principle always occur at a number of different points. It may take a long time before a firm conviction emerges as to the best point of revision.

Let us address ourselves to a familiar special case of the above question. What happens when incompatibility emerges for the Christian scholar between the results of science and what he regards as the belief-content of his authentic commitment? The possibilities of revision are two: he can revise his scientific views, even to the extent of setting out to reconstruct some branch of science; or he can revise his view as to what constitutes the belief-content of his authentic commitment, thereby also revising his actual commitment. For some time it may be unclear which of these is preferable. Even after it has become clear which is preferable, it may remain unclear how best to carry out his revisionary goal.

Historically, Christians have chosen the latter recourse again and again. As we saw in the preceding section, developments in dogmatic and biblical theology have repeatedly produced incompatibilities between what Christians regard as the results of science and what they regard as the belief-content of their authentic commitment. To resolve these, they have repeatedly adopted the strategy of revising their view as to what constitutes authentic commitment. They have followed the course of *harmonizing* their commitment with the results of theological science. The point can be generalized. Developments in science generally have induced people to revise their views as to what constitutes authentic commitment, and thus to revise their actual Christian commitment. In the extreme case people have given up their Christian commitment entirely. In less extreme cases they have resolved the incompatibility by some revision internal to the content of their commitment. And in principle the revision which resolves the incompatibility can always be made at a number of different points.[46]

That, I say, is how things have gone. And it seems beyond doubt that at least sometimes that is how they should have gone. Sometimes an incompatibility between what the Christian scholar regards as the results of science and what he regards as the

belief-content of his authentic commitment, can best
be resolved by the Christian's revising his beliefs on
the latter, for he may have been mistaken as to what
constitutes the belief-content of his authentic commitment.

So far I have been pressing the point that the
Christian in the practice of scholarship ought to let
the belief-content of his authentic commitment function as control over his theory-weighing. My em-
phasis here is almost the opposite. Sometimes he
should allow scientific developments to induce revisions in *what he views as* his authentic Christian
commitment. To revert to our original example, the
Congregation of the Inquisition viewed the geocentric theory as belonging to authentic commitment. I
think they were mistaken, and virtually the entire
community of Christians now thinks they were mistaken. We have all revised our beliefs, though we
have by no means all revised them at the same point.
What originally induced the revisions were developments in astronomy and physics. Thus it must
be concluded that developments in science have induced at least some of us to move toward a better
view as to what constitutes authentic Christian
commitment—if you assume (as I do) that at least
some of the revisions constitute a better view.

Sometimes the relation between theory and
commitment has been described in such a way as to
make it appear impossible that one's devising and
weighing of theories would ever have an influence
on one's commitment. It is said that religious belief

is *pre*-theoretical. Though religious belief can shape our devising and weighing of theories, it is proposed that our theories cannot shape our belief. This seems to me factually mistaken. The history of thought is replete with cases in which someone's view as to what constitutes authentic commitment was revised in the light of theoretical developments.

We have seen that Christians have been alarmed that theological developments have repeatedly induced revisions in people's view as to what constitutes their authentic commitment. The alarm has been just as great that developments in, say, physics and psychology have induced such revisions. And so, as we have seen, people have sought to prevent such revisions from occurring in the future to them and their particular subcommunities. I must say once again that I regard all such attempts as hopeless: there is no way to prevent such occurrences. I also regard such attempts as misguided. For though I would be among the last to minimize the dangers to a person's commitment to Christ in such developments, no one can deny that some of the revisions were justified. Christians have been mistaken in what they thought constituted authentic Christ-following; and sometimes they have become aware of their mistake through developments in science. Though authentic commitment ought to function as control within our theory-devising and theory-weighing, such activities will forever bear within them the potential for inducing, and for *justifiably* inducing, revisions in our views as to what constitutes authentic commitment, and thus, revisions in our actual commitment.

I have spoken thus far of revisions induced in our actual commitment, and in our views as to what constitutes authentic commitment, by scientific developments. And I have said that some such revisions are justifiably induced. A question which naturally comes to mind is whether scientific developments can produce changes in one's authentic commitment. Can it be that scientific developments change how one's following of Christ *ought* to be actualized—change what one *ought* to be doing and believing? This, I suppose, is the ultimately alarming possibility. But I think the answer must be Yes. For example, as a result of what we now know about the way in which mercury is stored up in fish, and the way in which when ingested it affects the human organism, it is probably the case that if we as Christians are to be consistent in our beliefs we must cease to allow mercury to be poured into the world's streams. It is probably the case that if we act otherwise, we are defecting from our authentic commitment.

The scholar never fully knows in advance where his line of thought will lead him. For the Christian to undertake scholarship is to undertake a course of action that may lead him into the painful process of revising his actual Christian commitment, sorting through his beliefs, and discarding some from a position where they can any longer function as control.[47] It may, indeed, even lead him to a point where

his authentic commitment has undergone change.
We are all profoundly *historical* creatures.

14/ Is faith a condition for knowledge?

The theory I have presented concerning the proper relation of Christian commitment to the devising and weighing of theories is obviously not a complementarist theory. The belief-content of one's authentic commitment is not seen as merely providing a complement of truths to those which can be derived from foundational certitudes.

But our theory is not clearly a preconditionalist one either. It is not clear that being a follower of Christ, exhibiting authentic commitment, and allowing the belief-content of that commitment to function as control within one's devising and weighing of theories are preconditions of arriving at a fully comprehensive, coherent, consistent, and true body of theories in the sciences. For as we have seen a theory which satisfies the control beliefs of a Christian may also satisfy those of some non-Christian. True theories may emerge from the use of false control beliefs. The preconditionalist is correct that there ought to be some internal relation between one's commitment and one's devising and weighing of theories, but that relation is not quite the simple one of true faith as a condition of true learning. A slight variant on true faith may possibly serve as well.

Neither of course is it the case that those who exhibit authentic commitment are thereby *guaranteed* of arriving at a wholly satisfactory body of theories. In fact none of us exhibits authentic commitment. But even if someone did exhibit such commitment, various alternative conflicting theories might jointly comport and be consistent with its belief-content. In addition, we have seen that not all theories can simply be extracted from the belief-content of one's authentic commitment. Many, if they are to be obtained at all, must be imaginatively devised. The requisite imagination may, however, be lacking in a person who exhibits authentic commitment. An additional factor is that not all of what belongs to the belief-content of one's authentic commitment may be true. Some of what God wishes us to believe may be fit and proper for us as his "children" to believe, yet strictly speaking false. For all we know this may lead to theories which, though fully satisfactory for our human purposes, are also strictly speaking false.

It must also be said, I think, that non-Christians, just by virtue of being such, have played an historically indispensable role in the growth of theory. In their opposition to what they knew as Christianity, they have sometimes explored lines of thought that proved fruitful and important. As I understand it, evolutionary theory in its early stages was developed mainly by scholars opposing what they saw as intrinsic to authentic Christian commitment. Looking back, those who have harmonized elements of evolutionary theory with their Christian commitment can say that those early theorizers were mistaken in their judgment as to what was intrinsic to authentic commitment. Maybe they were. But it would be incorrect to go on to argue that the harmonizing could have been accomplished then already, and that it was just as likely that evolutionary theory at its beginnings would have been developed by the Christian scholars of the day. That may be a *logical* possibility, but it seems to me an *historical* impossibility. The requisite motivations were lacking. Again, the behaviorist focuses attention on that part of man allied with the animals: his response to stimuli and susceptibility to operant conditioning. But the animal side of man's nature has traditionally been embarrassing and distasteful to Christians, something they would prefer not to focus on. Therefore, though it is a logical possibility that what is true in behaviorist theory could have been developed by Christians, it is doubtful that it is an historical possibility. Once again, the requisite motivations were lacking.

The Christian and the non-Christian alike accomplish God's purpose in history.

15/ *Some unanswered questions*

Two matters vitally important for our theory cannot be discussed here.

The first pertains to the Scriptures, and it consists itself of two large questions: how ought the Scriptures to be interpreted? (the question of *hermeneutics*); and how ought the Scriptures to function for the work of the Christian scholar? (the question of *authority*).

As we have seen, the Christian scholar is a member of a community which holds that the Scriptures ought to guide the life and thought of everyone committed to being a Christ-follower. Consequently the Bible ought to guide the scholar like all other members of the community in determining the belief-content of his authentic commitment. But how in detail do they do this? Even when we have settled hermeneutical questions, this difficult and complicated issue remains.

The fundamental source of the difficulty is that no one really believes that everything some biblical writer says, or presumes, ought to be believed. For example, no one reading these words believes that he ought to believe that the earth is flat and has four corners, though that is certainly what some biblical writers seem to presume. But if this is indeed said or presumed, why is it not taken as normative when other things said or presumed are so taken? How does one decide whether something said or presumed in Scripture is or is not normative for the belief-content of one's authentic Christian commitment?[48]

Secondly, we have not at all discussed the normative issue of whether, given one's beliefs at a certain time, there are some theories that one is warranted in accepting or in not accepting. Many have concluded from the collapse of foundationalism that there are no such warranted actions—that "anything goes." I disagree. Throughout this discussion I have presupposed that there are some theories that one is warranted in accepting or not accepting. I have repeatedly spoken of what the scholar *ought* to do. But to attempt to argue the case here would be well beyond my scope. Let me simply say that, given the collapse of foundationalism, the issue will have to be formulated as I have formulated it above: *Given such-and-such a body of beliefs,* is the scholar warranted in accepting or warranted in not accepting theory T? Warrant will have to be relative to a body of beliefs. It cannot be relative to a body of certitudes.

The normative question as to whether, given a body of beliefs B, one is warranted in accepting a theory T must be distinguished from what might be called the *heuristic* question as to whether one's acceptance of T or one's nonacceptance of T would contribute more to the ultimate goal for our devising and weighing of theories. This ultimate goal I understand as pretty much what Kant suggested—a consistent, coherent (i.e., not *ad hoc*), and comprehensive body of true theories. It may be that sometimes this goal would have been more rapidly advanced if theorists in some field had rejected a theory which they were warranted in accepting. Probably chemists were at one time eminently warranted in still accepting the phlogiston theory even though the goal for theorizing would have been more rapidly advanced if at that time they had all given it up.

It is only by looking back (if then) that we can tell what hindered and what advanced the goal for theorizing. It is never a question that we can with any confidence answer at the time. So if one confuses the normative issue with the heuristic issue—as I think many contemporary thinkers have done—one will naturally come to the skeptical conclusion that the issue of warrant is in fact an idle issue to raise.

Though with hindsight we may be able to pick out individual incidents which advanced the goal for theorizing and individual incidents which hindered it, it does not at all follow that we can formulate a *general heuristic*—a strategy that will always tell what is the most efficient way of arriving at the goal for theorizing. What seems in fact to have contributed to the growth of theory is the most astounding succession of human foibles, follies, and frailties. Perhaps it is true, as Lakatos has suggested, that what leads most efficiently to the advance of theorizing is *a proliferation of tenaciously held theories,* no matter what the motive for the proliferation or the tenacity. But at best this is a very rough generalization. *How* tenacious? And *how* proliferative?

Just as we may be able to spot incidents which have advanced the goal of theorizing and ones which have hindered it, without being able to formulate a general heuristic, so too we may be able to spot incidents of warranted acceptance of some theory and incidents of warranted nonacceptance of some theory without being able to formulate *general norms* for theory acceptance and nonacceptance. Our inability to find and formulate general norms does not merit the skeptical conclusions that there are no such general norms, or that we never know whether we are warranted in accepting or in not accepting some theory, or that the concept of warrant lacks all application to theory acceptance and nonacceptance.

It should be added that a person's theory of whether theory acceptance and nonacceptance is sometimes, at least, warranted is itself influenced by his control beliefs. We cannot at this point jump back onto some foundation. People no more agree on this matter than on any other. It is my own conviction that man throughout his existence is a responsible agent. This I view as a component in my authentic Christian commitment. And it is this which leads me to the conviction that sometimes we are warranted in accepting some theory and sometimes we are warranted in not accepting some theory.

16/ The need for theories which suggest research programs

We have focused our attention on the devising and weighing of theories. As already remarked, these are certainly not the only actions performed with respect to theories. To arrive at an adequate understanding of what takes place in the sciences we would also have to discuss the function of theories as suggesting and guiding research programs. It may be that scientists in fact expend more time and energy pursuing research programs suggested by theories than in devising and weighing theories.

Seldom, however, do the attempts of Christian scholars to "integrate faith and learning" suggest any research programs within the sciences. I consider this a sign either of a failure on the part of Christian scholars to see how their commitment can and should be related to theory-weighing, or of weakness of imagination. To make some comments at the beginning of a biology course to the effect that all biological reality has been created by God suggests nothing at all by way of any research program within biology. It consists merely of what I earlier called "setting within a Christian context."

A like criticism must be leveled against the

otherwise interesting essay by Dorothy Sayers, "Toward a Christian Aesthetic."[49] After making a plea for a Christian aesthetic, Sayers argues that what the Christian sees above all in the arts is an analogy between divine and human creative activity. The analogy is that just as God expresses himself in an image, so the artist expresses himself in an image. Even if this suggestion is true it has the serious defect that (so far as I can see) it goes nowhere. It suggests no lines of inquiry within the arts. It leads to no research program.

Christian scholarship will be a poor and paltry thing, worth little attention, until the Christian scholar, under the control of his authentic commitment, devises theories that lead to promising, interesting, fruitful, challenging lines of research.

17/ *The challenge*

The task of implementing the vision of the Christian scholar espoused in these pages is not a job for hacks. It requires, on the contrary, all the qualities of the competent, imaginative, and courageous scholar. To contribute to the development of theory, sometimes in defiance of the academic establishment, obviously requires such qualities. But equally, to discern that some part of the belief-content of one's authentic Christian commitment ought to be functioning as control within some particular piece of theory-development requires such qualities. For the connection does not always leap out. The belief-content of one's authentic Christian commitment is a wonderfully rich and complex structure, and ever again one discovers that some connection of commitment to theory has been missed by oneself as well as by one's predecessors.

I think there are two particular reasons why the relevance of some facet of our Christian commitment to our devising and weighing of theories often escapes us. The first is that many twentieth-century Christians scarcely see the world as Christians. Our indigenous patterns of thought are not those of Christianity but those induced by the scientific worldview. Perhaps it was not so at one time. Once men perhaps naturally saw the events of history as the encounter of God with men. But for us the belief-content of our Christian commitment is something we must constantly remind ourselves of. For us it is more a matter of decision than of perception. For us it does not function as the spectacles through which we see what happens.

And then, too, many of us know far too little of Christian theology and of Christian philosophy. Consequently, we fail to see the *pattern* of our authentic commitment and its wide ramifications. We see only pieces and snatches and miss the full relevance of our Christian commitment to our devising and weighing of theories. Or our scholarship becomes eccentric. We mistake and misinterpret the belief-content of our authentic commitment, we misplace emphases, alter the structure, distort. Where Christian theology and Christian philosophy are not in a healthy and robust state, or where their results are not widely diffused among scholars, I see little hope that the rest of Christian scholarship can be solid and vigorous. Christian philosophy and theology are at the center, not because they are infallible (obviously they're not), but because it is in these two disciplines that the Christian scholar engages in systematic self-examination.

Part II
THEORY AND PRAXIS

18/ *Learning for Shalom*

Two fundamental sorts of decisions face every scholar. He must decide which matters to investigate. And on the matters under investigation, he must decide which views to hold. In the first part of this book I addressed myself to the bearing of the Christian faith on the latter of these two sorts of issues. Here I address myself to the bearing of the Christian faith on the former, paying particular attention to the pure-versus-praxis-oriented-theory debate.

Deep in the Christian tradition is the conviction that each of us is not to be the center of his own concerns but is rather to love and serve God with all his life, and, in similar fashion, to love his neighbor as himself. One might add to these the conviction that each is also to be a responsible steward of the creation within which God has placed us. To love and serve God in all our ways, to love our neighbors as ourselves, and to be responsible stewards of nature— those are clearly proclaimed in the authoritative Scriptures of the Christian community as the fundamental obligations of mankind.

Deep in the Christian tradition is also the conviction that the fundamental attitude of God himself toward humanity is that of love. It would seem then that the goal God sets for human existence is intimately linked to the service, love, and stewardship he asks of us. It would seem that human fulfillment is to be found in what we experience when we love God with our whole life, when we love our neighbors as ourselves, when we act as responsible stewards of nature. It would seem that in enjoining us to act thus with respect to himself, neighbor, self, and nature, God is enjoining us to participate in his own cause of human fulfillment—to be his agents in the world. And I judge that the Christian Scriptures do indeed present the situation thus.

Yet there is within the Christian tradition a strange reluctance—even a refusal—thus to link what God sets as human responsibility and what he sets as the goal toward which he is working in history. For example, the Westminster divines would not disagree with what I have said concerning the fundamental character of human responsibility. Yet in the catechism they composed they said that the end of man is to know God and enjoy him forever. Notice, in this formulation, how nature and neighbor have dropped from the picture. The situation is basically no different if we look, for another example, at Aquinas. He too would not disagree with what I have said concerning the structure of human responsibility. Yet the *beatitudo* which he regarded as the end of human existence differs in its essential marks not at all from what the high Calvinists assembled at Westminster meant by knowing and enjoying God.

I have already suggested that the proclamation of the Christian Scriptures concerning God's goal for mankind is different. I shall try to say what, in my judgment, the goal is. Before I do so, however, it should be remarked that it is a goal which has the character of *renewal*. Our human situation is not such that a loving God would simply try to bring to fuller development all the tendencies already at work in self and society. For many of those tendencies lead to quite the opposite of love of God, self, and neighbor. They lead to deprivation and oppression. Renewal is needed.

To the question, "What is God's goal for human existence, to which human beings are called to contribute?" many of our brothers and sisters in the Third world, and in the oppressed components of the First and Second worlds, would today say "liberation." *Liberation* is what God's cause in the world is all about, and which you and I should then commit ourselves to. I can well appreciate why they speak thus. And yet I must say that this does not seem to me an adequate answer. For it leaves unanswered the question, "After liberation, then what?"

I suggest that immediately at hand in the Christian Scriptures is a better concept for describing God's goal for human existence. Admittedly it is a concept which has enjoyed only marginal attention in the Christian tradition. But it seems to me a concept well worth taking note of. The concept I have in mind is the concept of *peace*—in Hebrew, *shalom,* in Greek, *eirenē.*

The goal of human existence is that man should dwell at peace in all his relationships: with God, with himself, with his fellows, with nature, a peace which is not merely the absence of hostility, though certainly it is that, but a peace which at its highest is *enjoyment.* To dwell in shalom is to enjoy living before God, to enjoy living in nature, to enjoy living with one's fellows, to enjoy life with oneself. A condition of shalom is justice, and a component in justice is liberation from oppression. Never can there be shalom without justice. Yet shalom is more than justice. Justice can be grim. In shalom there is delight.

It comes as a surprise to us that the prophets, those of all the biblical writers who speak most emphatically and intensely about justice, are also the ones who speak most concretely and explicitly about shalom. Isaiah hears God speaking thus:

> **Then justice shall make its home in the**
> **   wilderness,**
> **and righteousness dwell in the grassland;**
> **when righteousness shall yield peace**
> **and its fruit be quietness and confidence for ever.**
> **Then my people shall live in a tranquil country,**
> **dwelling in peace, in houses full of ease.**
> **[Isaiah 32:16–18]**

And in the best known passage of all, Isaiah describes the anticipated shalom with a multiplicity of images of harmony, harmony among the animals, harmony between man and animal:

114

> Then a shoot shall grow from the stock of Jesse,
> and a branch shall spring from his roots.
> The spirit of the Lord shall rest upon him,
> a spirit of wisdom and understanding,
> a spirit of counsel and power,
> a spirit of knowledge and the fear of the Lord
> . . . .
> Then the wolf shall live with the sheep,
> and the leopard lie down with the kid;
> the calf and the young lion shall grow up together,
> and a little child shall lead them;
> the cow and the bear shall be friends,
> and their young shall lie down together.
> The lion shall eat straw like cattle;
> the infant shall play over the hole of the cobra,
> and the young child dance over the viper's nest.
>
> [Isaiah 11:1–2, 6–8]

That shoot of which Isaiah spoke is he of whom the angels sang in celebration of his birth: "Glory to God in highest heaven, and on earth his *peace* for men on whom his favor rests" (Luke 2:14). He is the one of whom the priest Zechariah said that he will "guide our feet into the way of *peace*" (Luke 1:79). He is the one of whom Simeon said, "This day, Master, thou givest thy servant his discharge in *peace;* now thy promise is fulfilled" (Luke 2:29). He is the one of whom Peter said that it was by him that God preached "good news of *peace*" to Israel (Acts 10:36). He is the one of whom Paul, speaking as a Jew to the Gentiles, said that "he came and preached *peace* to you who were far off and *peace* to those who were near by" (Eph. 2:17). He is in fact Jesus Christ, whom Isaiah called the "Prince of *peace*" (Isa. 9:6).

115

I suggest that if the activities of the scholar are to be justified, that justification must be found ultimately in the contribution of scholarship to the cause of justice-in-shalom. The vocation of the scholar, like the vocation of everyone else, is to serve that end.

19/ *Justifications for theorizing*

The debate which one immediately enters, when considering how the scholar should go about determining the direction of his inquiries, is the debate between the defenders of *pure theory* and the defenders of *praxis-oriented theory.* Probably everyone in the contemporary world holds that *some* praxis-oriented theory is legitimate. The debate, then, is between those who go all the way to hold that *only* praxis-oriented theory is permissible, and those who, though allowing for the legitimacy of some praxis-oriented theory, are yet persuaded that it is important to have a significant number of scholars engaging in pure theory. (Many of these latter would go on to emphasize what they see as the danger of allowing into the academy those engaged in praxis-oriented theory.)

But what *is* pure theory? And what, correspondingly, is praxis-oriented theory?

In his now well-known Inaugural Address at Frankfurt (1965), Jürgen Habermas remarked that:

> **The word "theory" has religious origins. The** *theoros* **was the representative sent by Greek**

117

cities to public celebrations. Through *theoria*, that is through looking on, he abandoned himself to the sacred events. In philosophical language, *theoria* was transferred to contemplation of the cosmos. In this form, theory already presupposed the demarcation between Being and time that is the foundation of ontology. This separation is first found in the poem of Parmenides and returns in Plato's *Timaeus*. It reserves to *logos* a realm of being purged of inconstancy and uncertainty and leaves to *doxa* the realm of the mutable and perishable. When the philosopher views the immortal order, he cannot help bringing himself into accord with the proportions, which he sees in the motions of nature and the harmonic series of music, within himself; he forms himself through mimesis. Through the soul's likening itself to the motion of the cosmos, theory enters the conduct of life.[1]

To the best of my knowledge, it was among the Pythagoreans that the conviction first emerged that the attainment of theoretical knowledge inherently has the effect of improving the character of the theorizer, and that, accordingly, this is a justification for engaging in the pursuit of such knowledge. We may accordingly give the title of *Pythagorean justification* to the justification of theoretical inquiry by reference to the self-improvement that inherently results from gaining theoretical knowledge.[2]

A variant of the Pythagorean justification has its proponents yet today. Few persons any longer hold that the business of the theorizer is to contemplate the eternal order of the cosmos, thereby to have his soul ordered in imitation of the order contemplated. One does hear it said, though, that scholarship, by virtue of its methodology if not its results, frees its practitioners from prejudice, makes them more tolerant human beings, and gives them a "scientific" cast of mind. And quite clearly this can be regarded as a variant on the Pythagorean justification. According to this variant, it matters not at all whether any theoretical knowledge is actually attained. What counts is the pursuit. The process, not the product, produces self-improvement—inherently so.

In his Inaugural Address, Habermas suggests strongly that only the Pythagorean justification for theoretical inquiry is to be found in the pre-modern history of the West. And since he himself holds that learning is to be justified solely by the utility of its results for achieving various ends other than states of knowledge, he uses his telling of the history to suggest that his own position is faithful to the grand tradition of the West, whereas those who defend "pure theory" have departed from it. In my judgment this is a highly selective reading of the history. There is another tradition in the West, equally massive, which holds that some learning at least is justified by the inherent worth of the cognitive states which result and not merely by the worth of the effects flowing from them. To cite but two examples, this was the view of Augustine and of Thomas Aquinas. Let me call it, for the sake of convenience, the *Aquinian justification*. This is the justification of theoretical inquiry by reference to the inherent worth of the cognitive states achieved.

It is important to note that a person who holds that certain cognitive states of consciousness are of inherent worth need not hold that all such states are of *equal* worth. Some may be of more value than others. Clearly that was also the view of Augustine and Aquinas. Both held that knowing the eternal is of more worth than knowing the temporal. Augustine remarks that "if therefore this is the right distinction between wisdom and knowledge, that the intellectual cognition of eternal things pertains to wisdom, but the rational cognition of temporal things to knowledge, it is not difficult to judge which is to be esteemed more and which less. . . . The former is to be preferred to the latter."[3] And Aquinas confirms his adherence to this line of thought when he says, "The greatness of a virtue, as to its species, is taken from its object. Now the object of wisdom surpasses the objects of all the intellectual virtues: because wisdom considers the Supreme Cause, which is God. . . ."[4]

On this matter of the relative worth of cognitive states of consciousness Immanuel Kant offered what has become an influential version of the Aquinian justification. Quite clearly Kant sided with Aquinas in regarding the pursuit of at least some theoretical knowledge as justified by the inherent worth of the knowledge attained. Likewise he held that within the body of knowledge which is of inherent worth, some is more worth knowing than other. But he did not locate the superiority in the *object* of knowledge, in the thing known. And in particular, he did not hold that knowledge of God is superior to knowledge of what is not God, nor that knowledge of the transcendent eternal in general is superior to knowledge of the temporal. For he held that we can have no knowledge of God, nor any of the transcendent eternal.

On Kant's view, the superiority of certain forms of knowledge is to be located in the *formal characteristics* of that knowledge. It is *completeness of explanation* and *systematic unity* that are the great desiderata in knowledge. Characteristic of human nature is an impulse toward the pursuit of ever greater completeness of explanation, and ever greater systematic unity, in the body of our collective knowledge. And this impulse, Kant obviously believes, is beneficent; the more complete and unified a body of knowledge, so far forth the better. To suppose, though, that there can actually *be* a body of knowledge in which there are no remnants of incompleteness and disunity would be to suffer from illusion. There is no harm, perhaps there is even some benefit, in holding out before us as a luring vision the *prospect* of such a body of knowledge. But in fact we will never be in any other situation than that of striving for something *more* complex and *more* unified than what we have. Our lot is cast inevitably with the comparative. The superlative is forever beyond us.

This Kantian version of the Aquinian justification has gripped the conviction of many if not most scholars in the Western world. The perennial pursuit of mankind of a body of theory more complete and more unified than that which at the moment we possess is seen as justified by the inherent worth of the knowledge attained. It is not necessary, for the pursuit to be justified, that the knowledge attained prove useful.

I have classified this Kantian vision of the place of theorizing in human life as a version of the Aquinian justification, on the ground that it affirms the inherent worth of knowledge. At the same time, I have emphasized the radical difference between this version and Aquinas's own. No object is given preferential status in knowledge. Instead, preferential status is given to knowledge possessing certain *formal characteristics*. There is yet another difference worth noting. The ultimate goal of the scholar, says Aquinas, is that *he* the scholar will have knowledge of God. No doubt the scholar, out of charity for his fellows, will seek to share his knowledge. But the picture Aquinas has in mind is not that each scholar will make his contribution to a body of human knowledge, and that this will include the knowledge by *somebody or other* of God. The goal of *each* scholar is that *he* himself will attain to knowledge of God. Kant's picture is profoundly different. Here the goal is that each of us will contribute to a body of human knowledge which is an advance, with respect to completeness and unity, on what we have presently. But in fact no single person will ever have that better body of knowledge. It will be parcelled out across the community of scholars. The body of knowledge that any given scholar has will always be radically incomplete and lacking full coherence with knowledge possessed by the other scholars. There now exists a body of propositions each known by someone or other; and the goal of the scholar is to contribute to the formation of a new body of propositions, each known *by someone or other,* and such that the totality has greater completeness and unity than the present totality. But no one scholar will ever survey the whole of this edifice that together the community of scholars is building. All together are perennially engaged in building an edifice of which no one will ever see more than a tiny corner. And it may just be that the corner on which a given scholar works and which he surveys shows, during his lifetime, no increase in completeness and unity. The cognitive states he does have may nonetheless be of intrinsic worth to him. But they will be inferior to those he aimed to have, and to those which others will some day have, perhaps as the result of his contributions.

The English Renaissance writer Francis Bacon gave expression to yet a third influential line of thought concerning the justification of theorizing. "Knowledge is power," said Bacon. And clearly he thought that, for much knowledge, its value lies in its power. The justification of the pursuit of theoretical knowledge lies in the power placed in our hands by the cognitive states attained.

The power Bacon had in mind was power over one's circumstances. The cognitive results of scholarship are of use in altering one's circumstances to conform to one's desires. The model of action which Bacon probably had in mind was this: Having it as my goal to bring about B, and believing that by doing A I will bring about B, I do A. And probably it was his view that scholarship can both provide the *beliefs* on the basis of which we act, and suggest new *goals* for which to act.

The *Baconian justification* is like the Pythagorean in citing, as justification for the pursuit of theoretical knowledge, the utility of such knowledge for achieving various noncognitive benefits. It differs, though, in its identification of the relevant benefits. On the Pythagorean justification, the benefit which the attainment of theoretical knowledge yields is the moral benefit of altering the theorist's character for the better. And it was the conviction of the Pythagorean tradition that the practice of (the appropriate kind of) learning inherently yields this moral benefit. On the Baconian justification, the relevant benefit which the attainment of theoretical knowledge yields is the benefit of enabling us to alter our *circumstances*—the attainment of power. But this power is not thought of as *inherently* some good thing. Rather, the power in turn gets its justification *by actually being used* to alter one's circumstances in one way or another. The satisfaction of the Baconian justification requires that the results of learning be embedded within informed action. Learning is for action—action extrinsic to the action of learning. If learning is to be justified its results must be used in technology. And whether they are so used is a matter lying outside the hands of the scholar *qua* scholar.

The Baconian justification has of course so firmly gripped the conviction of Western man that today it has expanded far beyond what Bacon himself ever envisaged. It was principally alterations in our *physical* circumstances that Bacon had in mind when he suggested that the pursuit of knowledge is justified by the utility of its results for power. The pursuit of what might be called *technical* knowledge is what he urged. We in the twentieth century, having become aware of laws pertaining to *human* behavior and action, have seen the prospect of *behavioral* knowledge opening up before us, that is, of knowledge put to use in altering the actions of our fellow human beings in accord with our goals. Where previously an alliance existed between the researcher and the technologist of nature, now there also exists an alliance between the researcher and the technologist of society.[5]

In summary, in the West one finds a long history of those who affirm that scholarship is justified by the value of the noncognitive effects and utility of the knowledge attained; but also one finds a long history of those who hold that some of it at least is justified simply by the inherent value of the cognitive states of consciousness it yields. Of course these positions are not incompatible. Not only may one branch of inquiry be justified by reference to one of such justifications and another, by reference to another; but even a single branch of inquiry may be justified in both ways. Some matters of knowledge may be worth having both for their intrinsic worth, and for the sake of their inherent effects or utility.

Now it seems to me obvious—too obvious to need arguing—that for lifting the burdens of deprivation and oppression and advancing the cause of shalom, theoretical knowledge is useful. It is, in fact, *necessary*. The Christian understanding of the scholar's vocation clearly leads to the conclusion that the pursuit of at least some theoretical knowledge is justified by its results and its utility.

The interesting question, though, is whether that is the whole of the matter. Is the acquisition of theoretical knowledge to be justified *solely* by reference to the effects and utility of knowledge? Or could it be that the having and the acquisition of knowledge is itself a good thing? Could it be that it is itself a dimension of shalom, a component in human fulfillment?

Man's shalom, according to the witness of the Old Testament prophets, includes justice for the widow and the orphan. It includes as well the love between parents and children, and delight in green pastures and flowing brooks. Does it also include theoretical knowledge—the understanding of man, the universe, and God that scholarship can give us?

I find it impossible to answer no to this question. To me it seems evident that understanding, comprehension, knowledge, constitutes a fulfillment of our created nature. To me it seems evident that human fulfillment is less than God meant it to be insofar as there is ignorance in place of understanding, bewilderment in place of comprehension. Of course human fulfillment does not consist exclusively of knowledge. And of course there is more to comprehension and understanding than the theorist provides us with. Further, over and over we discover that rich interconnections of creation are such that knowledge has noncognitive benefits and uses. Yet I want to say that a theoretical comprehension of ourselves and of the reality in the midst of which we live—of its unifying structure and its explanatory principles—is a component in the shalom God meant for us. Where knowledge is absent, life is withered.

Knowledge—*some* knowledge, anyway—is of inherent worth, in that it constitutes a component in our God-appointed fulfillment. The Aquinian justification points to something real. Man is created a wondering creature, unfulfilled until his wonder finds fulfillment in knowledge.

20/ Choice-principles for the scholar

Our goal has been to get at the root of the pure theory/praxis-oriented theory debate. We are not yet there. For that debate, though it has a good deal to do with the issue of justification, is not directly *about* the proper justification of theorizing. Justifications of theorizing operate, as it were, on a "second level." The person who offers such a justification first surveys the field of theorizing, and then gives an account of its benefits. But the pure theory/praxis-oriented theory debate pertains to scholars operating on the *first* level. It pertains to the principles on which they should choose the direction of their investigations—to what I shall call their "choice-principles."

If we are to formulate with clarity the issues here, we must keep in mind these two different levels: the primary level of choice-principle, and the secondary level of justification. But of course, what one believes concerning justification has *bearing* on what one recommends concerning choice-principles.

The person who adopts the Aquinian justification holds that certain cognitive states of consciousness are of inherent worth. Thereby he has available to him a choice-principle for determining the direction of his inquiries, a *cognitive* choice-principle: choose those directions of inquiry which hold the greatest promise of yielding cognitive states of intrinsic worth. And if he also holds that intrinsically worthwhile states of knowledge differ among themselves with respect to their worth, then in turn he has available to him a cognitive choice-principle for choosing *among* such states: choose those directions of inquiry which hold the greatest promise of yielding knowledge of greatest inherent worth for the greatest number of people.[6]

And now I can introduce the notion of *pure theory*. When the direction of inquiry that a scholar follows has been chosen by him for the reason that he judged it held promise of yielding knowledge of inherent worth, let us say that he is then engaged in *pure theory*. I think that very often what people mean when they speak of someone as engaged in pure theory is exactly this. By contrast, when the direction of inquiry that a scholar follows has been chosen by him for the reason that he judged it held promise of yielding knowledge resulting in, or useful for, something other than cognitive states, let us say that he is engaged in *praxis-oriented theory*.[7]

However, not all who affirm the importance of pure theory mean by "pure theory" what I have just suggested. For some of these deny that cognitive states of consciousness have any inherent worth. If asked to give a justification for theoretical inquiry they might offer a Baconian theory, but certainly not an Aquinian one. Yet they affirm the importance of theorizing which is not praxis-oriented.

On first hearing, that is simply bewildering. How can someone hold that scholarship is justified exclusively by its utility in altering our circumstances in desirable ways, and at the same time recommend theorizing which is not praxis-oriented? What the Baconian justification straightforwardly yields is some such (noncognitive) choice-principle as this: Choose those directions of inquiry which hold the greatest promise of yielding knowledge useful in altering our human circumstances in the most desirable ways. But if one does in fact choose a direction of inquiry solely on this principle, then one is engaged in praxis-oriented theory. So how can one combine the Baconian justification for learning with insistence on the importance of theorizing which is not praxis-oriented?[8]

In the following way: by claiming that more technologically beneficial knowledge is likely to result if there are a number of researchers who direct their investigations with no regard to technological benefit. It is argued that if everyone directed his research along lines that he judged beneficial to the Department of Defense, the National Park Service, the Department of Health and Human Services, etc., the long-range technological interests of mankind would be poorly served. In short, there is abroad in the contemporary world a confidence in the existence of a preestablished harmony between results that emerge from theory which is not praxis-oriented and those that in the long run are the most technologically beneficial.

But how then does such a person recommend that

the scholar determine the direction of his inquiry—a person, that is, who holds that the worth of knowledge lies exclusively in its noncognitive benefits, while yet believing that some researchers should avoid engaging in praxis-oriented theorizing? What choice-principle does he advocate? For choice there must be.

I think that most of those who think along the lines suggested would say this: the best way to serve the technological interests of mankind is to allow a sizeable body of researchers to pursue whatever matters they find of greatest intellectual interest to themselves. And theorizing thus pursued is what some have in mind by "pure theory."

So I suggest that two rather different understandings of "pure theory" are present in the contemporary world. Some mean by "pure theory" theorizing whose direction was chosen for the reason that the researcher judged it would yield knowledge of inherent worth. That is how I defined "pure theory" a few pages back. Call it, now *objective* pure theory. Others mean by "pure theory" theorizing whose direction was chosen for the reason that the researcher judged it would prove intellectually interesting to himself. *Subjective* pure theory, we might call this.[9]

And now what does the Christian, who holds that it is the calling of the scholar to serve God's cause of justice-in-shalom, have to say about the pure theory/praxis-oriented theory debate? What does he recommend for the scholar's choice-principle?

He will not say that in principle only praxis-oriented theory is legitimate. Accordingly, he cannot simply adopt the principle: Choose whichever direction of inquiry holds the greatest promise of yielding results or utility of greatest worth to the greatest number of people. For he holds, as I have argued, that at least *some* knowledge is of intrinsic worth. And that conviction will enter into his calculations as to which line of investigation to pursue.[10]

So how about the other way around: can he hold that in principle only pure theory is legitimate? Well, earlier I remarked on the necessity of theoretical knowledge for informed praxis. So if one held, nevertheless, that the theorist in determining the direction of his inquiries should never have his eye on practice, should always engage exclusively in pure theory, that position would have to be defended by holding to the preestablished harmony notion that always the best way for the theorist to serve the interest of praxis is to engage in pure theory.[11]

Now it's true, of course, that over and over knowledge acquired in the course of pure theory has in fact turned out to have some important practical applications. And sometimes it looks unlikely that the knowledge would have emerged if all scholars had been engaged only in praxis-oriented theory. But at the same time, what also turns out over and over is that the theoretical knowledge we need to accomplish some practical goal proves to be missing. Accordingly, we find that we have to acquire it in service of that goal. We have to engage in praxis-oriented theory. The point is so crucial as to merit repetition: *repeatedly the knowledge we need for our noncognitive goals proves not to have emerged from pure theory.* As thinkers from the Third World have recently suggested, First World theorizing has contributed no significant intellectual resources to their goals of social reform, suggesting thereby that our Western "pure theory" is in fact not very pure, but is far more oriented to preserving our own social order than we like to think. In any case, I think it decisively clear that in principle, praxis-oriented theory is legitimate. We cannot assume that always the best way to serve praxis is to engage in pure theory.

So where does that leave us? It leaves us in the position of saying to the scholar that since both the intrinsic worth of knowledge and the beneficial results and utility of knowledge have legitimate claims on him, he will have to assess the priority of the one over against the other. He cannot engage in praxis-oriented theory without first considering the claims of knowledge which is of intrinsic worth; and he cannot engage in pure theory without first considering the claims of the inherent results and utility of knowledge. The scholar cannot operate exclusively with the choice-principle of selecting whatever direction of inquiry holds most promise of yielding knowledge of greatest inherent worth. But neither can he operate exclusively with the choice-principle of selecting whatever direction holds most promise of yielding knowledge of use for the noncognitive concerns of greatest worth. Always he must engage in the difficult and complex task of weighing the one against the other, pure theory against praxis-oriented theory, deciding which holds most promise of contributing most substantially to the cause of justice-in-shalom.

And always he must do so in the light of his own concrete historical and cultural situation, and in the light of his own capacities. He cannot give an abstract, once-for-all answer. The needs of mankind for knowledge are different in one place and time from what they are in another. They are different in South America from what they are in North America. Responsible scholarship always bears the marks of its time and place of birth.

Thus I find I cannot agree with the South American scholar Hugo Assmann, whom Miguez-Bonino quotes as rejecting "any *logos* which is not the logos of a *praxis*." [12] But equally I cannot give my approval to those scholars in the Western world who simply assume without question that they are justified in pursuing a *logos* which is not the *logos* of any *praxis*. If the scholar is to act responsibly, he cannot evade the difficult task of ascertaining priorities in his concrete situation. Yet Assmann's words have their point. For the scholar in the West is more often found to be irresponsibly ignoring the claims of praxis-oriented theory than he is found to be irresponsibly ignoring the claims of pure theory. So, for example, in the midst of the existential bewilderment of Americans as to the criteria for a just war, most of our scholars continued their pursuit of pure theory.

One thing more must be said here. A few pages back I distinguished between objective pure theory and subjective pure theory—that is, between theorizing pursued for the intrinsic worth of the knowledge it promises to yield, and theorizing pursued for the intellectual interest it promises to the researcher. Now the responsible scholar, I am persuaded, can never be content to pursue a line of investigation simply because it promises to be interesting to him. Of course he hopes that it will prove interesting. And he acknowledges that part at least of what gives worth to knowledge is that it proves of interest to human beings. But that some line of inquiry promises to be interesting, whether or not it is important, and then interesting just to him, perhaps to no one else, cannot all by itself ever be his decisive reason for pursuing it. He cannot put out of mind considerations of worth— and more specifically considerations pertaining to what is of worth for his fellow human beings generally, not just to himself.

21 / *Two alternative views*

(1) Augustine and Aquinas did not hold merely that knowledge of the eternal God is that form of knowledge which is of greatest inherent worth. They held that knowledge of the eternal God is the noblest of all such inherently worthwhile ends—not merely the noblest of all forms of knowledge but the noblest of all human ends. Further, it was their view that knowledge of God can, in part, be gained by way of theoretical reflection.[13] On their view, accordingly, the pursuit of knowledge of the eternal God is the noblest activity available to a human being.[14]

Let us see briefly how this position is worked out by Aquinas. The true end (goal) of man, says Aquinas, is happiness. And "man's happiness consists essentially in his being united to the Uncreated Good. . . ."[15] Thus "the ultimate and principal good of man is the enjoyment of God. . . ."[16]

Now the essence of this union with God which constitutes man's ultimate happiness "consists in an act of the intellect. . . ."[17] Specifically, man's ultimate happiness consists in the intellectual act of knowing God in his essence.[18] The goal of achieving that happiness does, or should, govern our will; so one might say that "the delight that results from happiness pertains to the will."[19] But nonetheless the goal *consists* in an act of the intellect.

But why should it be supposed that knowing God—and incidentally, we may give the title of *wisdom* to such knowledge—why should it be supposed that knowing God is man's ultimate end? Why should it be thought that in wisdom lies man's ultimate beatitude? Because

> **if man's happiness is an operation, it must need be man's highest operation. Now man's highest operation is that of his highest power in respect of its highest object: and his highest power is the intellect, whose highest object is the Divine Good, which is the object, not of the practical, but of the speculative intellect. Consequently happiness consists principally in such an operation, viz., in the contemplation of Divine things. . . . Therefore the last and perfect happiness which we await in the life to come, consists entirely in contemplation. But imperfect happiness, such as can be had here, consists first and principally in contemplation, but secondarily, in an operation of the practical intellect directing human actions and passions[20]**

"Perfect and true happiness cannot be had in this life. . . ." Nonetheless, "a certain participation of Happiness can be had in this life. . . ."[21] "In so far as a man gives himself to the pursuit of wisdom, so far does he even now have some share in true beatitude."[22]

If wisdom constitutes the essence of man's ultimate happiness, how then does the "theological virtue" of charity fit into the picture? Well, charity may be defined as "the friendship of man for God,"[23] and the actualization of this virtue is then man's love for God. It may be said about charity that "since charity attains God, it unites us to God. . . ."[24] Now "likeness causes love. . . ."[25] And it is through the pursuit of wisdom that man "especially approaches to a likeness to God who 'made all things in wisdom.' And since likeness is the cause of love, the pursuit of wisdom especially joins man to God in friendship."[26] So it may be concluded that charity is an inherent result of that unity with God established by wisdom—that is, by knowing God.

But if the essence of human happiness consists just in an intellectual contemplation of God, is there then no need for human companionship in man's ultimate end? And is there no need for delight in nature? Is the existence of a just and happy community dwelling in harmony with nature just irrelevant to man's ultimate happiness?

Not perhaps irrelevant. But certainly unnecessary. Here in this life the happy man needs friends, and needs what will sustain the body.[27] But not so when he has attained perfect happiness. In the intellectual contemplation of God there will be no lack whatsoever. "If we speak of perfect Happiness, which will be in our heavenly Fatherland, the fellowship of friends is not essential to Happiness, since man has the entire fullness of his perfection in God."[28] Should we find ourselves in the presence of other human beings, love for them will result from love for God. Then friendship will be "as it were, concomitant with perfect Happiness."[29] But the absence of human companionship will mean no deficiency in fulfillment. Likewise, the person who when disembodied has knowledge of God experiences no deficiency. "Since man's perfect Happiness consists in the vision of the Divine Essence, it does not depend on the body. Consequently, without the body the soul can be happy."[30] The person who knows and loves God will eventually receive a new body at the resurrection. He will then experience an increase in the extent of his happiness. However, he will experience no increase in its intensity.[31] And even then it should be added that the body to which his soul will be united will be "no longer animal but spiritual. Consequently [the] external goods [of our present bodies] are nowise necessary for that Happiness, since they are ordained to the animal life. . . ."[32]

Obviously this is a profoundly different perspective from that which I have outlined, yielding a view as to the proper relation of theorizing to human life generally which differs on very many points indeed. Let me call attention to just one difference, a difference which does not spring at once to view. Not every human being can be a scholar, be it for lack of time, of ability, or of inclination. Accordingly, what follows immediately from the Thomistic view is intellectual elitism. Learning in its highest form is for the benefit of the scholars themselves, lifting them up to a state of being higher than that of their fellows. The others remain outside, looking in, deriving at best vicarious benefit. To enter the world of theory is to leave behind what is inferior in end and action. It is to be freed, to be liberated, from the flickering gloom of the cave for the bright light of the sun. And only *some* can be freed. By contrast, in the position which I developed, scholarship is placed directly in the service of mankind.

(2) A thoroughly nonelitist view of scholarship was espoused in an alternative view on the relation of learning to life—what might be called the *traditional Protestant view*. Reading their Old Testaments, the Protestants, and particularly the Calvinist Protestants, were struck by the "dominion" passages: subdue the earth and have dominion. They heard in these the message that humanity has a mandate from God—a "cultural mandate," as it came eventually to be called. Perhaps a plausible surface reading of the "dominion" words of the Old Testament is that man is there enjoined to engage in what Marx eventually called "productive labor." But that is not the way the Protestant tradition characteristically understood them. It understood them as enjoining not only productive labor but the whole formation of culture. And it understood the development of scholarship as an essential component in cultural formation—not just as an instrument for self-improvement, and not just as an instrument for beneficial alteration of one's circumstances, but as something good in its own right. God has declared it such, and enjoined its pursuit, so

that it is part of man's obedient response to the cultural mandate.

But naturally it constitutes only one phase of man's total response. And the reformers saw no reason whatsoever for thinking it the noblest. Every occupation is to be a vocation before the face of God, each equal in nobility, if not in strategic importance, with the other. In God's sight learning is no more noble than farming, theorizing no more noble than cabinetmaking, scholarship than politics. All legitimate occupations have the same status before God of being obedient responses to the cultural mandate. Elitism has been struck dead.

Yet some essential emphases are curiously missing here. What is emphasized is our calling to humanize the world. What is missing is the insistence that such humanizing is never to be done merely to place the print of our hands and minds upon nature, but always for human benefit. What is missing is the note that each person is to work for the benefit of his fellow human beings. That the scholar must consider the needs of his fellow human beings in directing his scholarship is never recognized.

What is also curiously missing is the theme of fall and renewal. The stress is all on man's *creaturely* calling to humanize the world. To that peculiar reorientation in our responsibilities which occurred when man fell and God set about to work for renewal, no attention is given. And thus that *particular* mode of the scholar's service to his fellow human beings which consists in his aiding in the cause of lifting the burdens of deprivation and oppression imposed by his fellow human beings goes unnoticed. What I have argued by contrast is that a scholar's inquiries must take their course in the light of the fallen condition of our actual society. Intellectual culture is never to be severed from the deprivations and oppressions to be found in our actual social conditions. One cannot proceed as if we lived within a society which is pristine and unfallen, whose only deficiency is that it is not yet fully developed.

Further, there is a curious abstractness, a curious ahistorical quality, to the Protestant view. There is no sense of the seesaw battle taking place in history between forces that advance and forces that retard the coming of shalom, with the consequent necessity for the scholar to choose his strategic point of entry. In lordly fashion the scholar remains above the strife, "developing culture," writing his books while the Reichstag burns.

I think it must be said that the Protestant view, by virtue of ignoring these factors, has all too often encouraged the irresponsible pursuit of pure theory when praxis-oriented theory was called for. Thinking himself fully justified by the cultural mandate, the Protestant scholar all too often ignored the priorities of God's cause of renewal, and simply pursued whatever knowledge he thought worth acquiring for its own sake. True, he did not think that thereby he was doing something better than his fellows who were not scholars. But also he did not ask how he could enable them better to do what they were doing. And in particular, he acted as if cultural fulfillment could be attained without intermingling the struggle for fulfillment with the struggle for lifting the bonds of deprivation and oppression. Culture was removed from history and from society, and treated as a "world" of its own.

22 / *A concluding objection*

Objections to what I have said arise from all sides.
Prominent among them is the claim that the existence
of pure theory is an illusion. No one ever does engage
in pure theory. Perhaps no one can. We delude
ourselves in thinking that we do. All theory is in fact
praxis-oriented. So it is said.

From the variety of reasons offered in support of
this position, among the most common is one which
makes use of Marx's thought. Those two great
modern masters in the art of suspecting,[33] Marx and
Freud, have taught us all to distinguish, on both the
individual and the social level, between the *genuine*
reasons for our actions and what we *offer* as reasons,
but which are in fact *rationalizations* for the genuine
reasons. We conceal from ourselves and others our
genuine reasons by throwing up smoke screens of
rationalization. The claim, then, is that if we
scrutinize those scholars who claim to be following
some direction of inquiry for the *reason* that they
judge it likely to lead to knowledge of inherent worth,
we will see that they are offering rationalizations for
their genuine reasons and not the genuine reasons

themselves. In fact, so it is said, the *true* reason for their choice is their belief that that line of inquiry will advance their own *self*-interest by perpetuating the position of privilege and power enjoyed by themselves and their class.

Unfortunately I do not here have the space to give this claim the full consideration it deserves. I must content myself with saying that I am not persuaded that this cynical reading of human motivation is invariably the correct one. Immediately I must go on to observe, however, that very often it is correct. The human heart is deeply deceitful; and to their great credit Marx and Freud have taught us much about its devious paths. Often it is true that the scholar who says and even believes that he is engaged in pure theory is in fact working to shore up a society in which he occupies a position of privilege and power. He enjoys his position by producing scholarship whose secret motivation is to perpetuate that position. (And even when that is not his genuine reason, it may nonetheless be the *consequence* of his choices.) Accordingly, a responsible decision by the scholar on the priority of pure theory vs. praxis-oriented theory requires that he become "self-conscious." And as to the path to self-consciousness, there is none better than that of listening attentively to the message of the Bible, that great unmasker of deceit, while at the same time listening attentively to the cries of those who make the claim of deprivation and oppression— Gentiles listening to Jews, Jews to Arabs, men to women, rich to poor, South African whites to South

African blacks, Dutchmen to Moluccans, North Americans to South Americans, the First World to the Third. The person who turns one of his ears to the prophetic unmasking word of the gospel and the other to the cries of those who suffer deprivation and oppression is not likely to suffer from the illusion that he is engaged in pure theory when in fact he is working to shore up his own position of privilege.

Notes

Notes to Part I

1. See Giorgio de Santillana, *The Crime of Galileo* (Chicago, 1955), esp. Chap. V.

2. For the tale of the Cartesian/Newtonian controversy, see for example Thomas Kuhn, *The Structure of Scientific Revolutions* (Chicago, 1962), pp. 103f. And for examples of religious/theological beliefs functioning as control in the seventeenth-century scientific disputes, see A. Koyre, *From the Closed World to the Infinite Universe* (Baltimore, 1957).

3. Discussed and quoted in Paul K. Feyerabend, "Philosophy of Science: A Subject with a Great Past," in *Minnesota Studies in the Philosophy of Science,* V (Minneapolis, 1970), p. 180.

4. An especially good telling of most of the tale is to be found in Carl G. Hempel, "The Empiricist Criterion of Meaning," reprinted in A. J. Ayer, *Logical Positivism* (Glencoe, Ill., 1959).

5. As to what I have in mind when I speak of theorizing, see the opening paragraphs of section 9. And as to why, in what follows, I usually speak of Christian *commitment* rather than of Christian *faith,* see fn. 34.

6. See for example Kuhn, *op. cit.,* throughout. And see Imre Lakatos, "Falsification and the Methodology of Scientific Research Programs," in Lakatos and Musgrave (eds.), *Criticism and the Growth of Knowledge* (Cambridge, 1970).

7. R. M. Hare, "Theology and Falsification," in Flew and MacIntyre (eds.), *New Essays in Philosophical Theology* (London, 1955), pp. 100f. For another classic example of the same general strategy see R. B. Braithwaite, "An Empiricist's View of the Nature of Religious Belief," in I. T. Ramsey (ed.), *Christian Ethics and Contemporary Philosophy* (London, 1966). For an example of

the same strategy practiced by a theologian rather than a philosopher see Paul van Buren, *The Secular Meaning of the Gospel* (New York, 1963).

8. An alternative formula would be this: *A person is warranted in accepting a theory at a certain time if and only if the theory then belongs to genuine science.* But this seems on the face of it unsatisfactory. For on this view if a person were to guess correctly that a theory belongs to genuine science, he would be warranted in accepting the theory.

9. On this understanding of "theory of genuine science," the body of scientific theory does not grow and expand. It is fixed, static. All that grows is our human knowledge of what belongs to genuine science. One might call this a *Platonic* concept of science. An alternative way of understanding "theory of genuine science" is this: *A theory T belongs to genuine science at some time t if and only if it is justified by some foundational proposition and some human being knows with certitude at or before t that T is thus justified.* (The definition of "foundational" must also be suitably revised from what stands in the text.) This might be called the *progressive* concept of science. When "theory of genuine science" is thus understood, a theory may at one time not belong to genuine science and may at a later time belong. To my knowledge, this distinction between Platonic science and progressive science is not made with any clarity in the foundationalist tradition. So I think it is impossible to say which concept has been dominant. I work with the concept of Platonic science in the text solely because if offers greater ease in exposition.

10. In the text I assume that the foundational propositions are those which can be known with certitude—and this is indeed what most foundationalists have held. But there are other possibilities, each allied with a concept closely similar to but not identical with that of certitude. For example, one might say that *a proposition is foundational for a given person if and only if there is no other proposition which he is more warranted in believing.* To further complicate the matter, we shall shortly see that "certitude" is itself a word attached to several different (though similar) concepts.

Another alternative concept of foundational to that which is found in the text is this: *A proposition is foundational if and only if it is true and every human being who entertained it in the appropriate circumstances would know noninferentially and with certitude that it is true.* Perhaps this is the concept that some foundationalists work with. However, the fundamental foundationalist vision is just that to be a theory of genuine science a proposition must be justified by reference to some certitude. Science must be erected on a secure foundation. It seems quite sufficient, for this vision, that the secure foundational propositions be true and be ones which *someone* could know with certitude to be true. To demand that all of them be ones which *any* human being, if he entertained them in the appropriate curcumstances, would know with certitude to be true, seems quite irrelevant.

11. Apparently Aquinas held, however, that they are known by God and the blessed—that they are self-evident to them or known to be demonstrable from what is self-evident. This thought enters into his insistence that theology, too, is a science. The theologian begins with revealed propositions and proceeds to construct demonstrations. Many of those revealed propositions are not self-evident to him. However, he is warranted in believing that they are known to the blessed (because he is warranted in believing Scripture and the church). Thus he is warranted in believing that they do belong to genuine science. Accordingly, when in the text I speak of Aquinas' view of properly conducted scientific inquiry, what I say is not, as it stands, true of the science of theology. It is true of all nontheological sciences, theology being a science of a special sort. See *Summa theologica* I,i,2.

12. Consider, for example, the following passages from Calvin's *Institutes*:

> For this reason, I have said that all parts of the soul were possessed by sin after Adam deserted the fountain of righteousness. For not only did a lower appetite seduce him, but unspeakable impiety occupied the very citadel of his mind, and pride penetrated to the depths of his heart. Thus it is pointless and foolish to restrict the corruption that arises thence only to what are called the impulses of the senses; or to call it the "kindling wood" that attracts, arouses, and drags into sin only that part which they term "sensuality."
>
> The whole third chapter of Romans is nothing but a description of original sin (vs. 1-20). From the "renewal" that fact appears more clearly. For the Spirit, who is opposed to the old man and to the flesh, not only marks the grace whereby the lower or sensual part of the soul is corrected, but embraces the full reformation of all the parts. Consequently, Paul not only enjoins that brute appetites be brought to nought but bids us "be renewed in the spirit of our mind" (Eph. 4:23); in another passage he

similarly urges us to "be transformed in newness of mind" (Rom. 12:2). From this it follows that that part in which the excellence and nobility of the soul especially shine has not only been wounded, but so corrupted that it needs to be healed and to put on a new nature as well. We shall soon see to what extent sin occupies both mind and heart. Here I only want to suggest briefly that the whole man is overwhelmed—as by a deluge—from head to foot, so that no part is immune from sin and all that proceeds from him is to be imputed to sin. As Paul says, all turnings of the thoughts to the flesh are enmities against God (Rom. 8:7), and are therefore death (Rom. 8:6) (II.ii.9).

Therefore, so that the order of discussion may proceed according to our original division of man's soul into understanding and will, let us first of all examine the power of the understanding. When we so condemn human understanding for its perpetual blindness as to leave it no perception of any object whatever, we not only go against God's Word, but also run counter to the experience of common sense. For we see implanted in human nature some sort of desire to search out the truth to which man would not at all aspire if he had not already savored it. Human understanding then possesses some power of perception, since it is by nature captivated by love of truth. The lack of this endowment in brute animals proves their nature gross and irrational. Yet this longing for truth, such as it is, languishes before it enters upon its race because it soon falls into vanity. Indeed, man's mind, because of its dullness, cannot hold to the right path, but wanders through various errors and stumbles repeatedly, as if it were groping in darkness, until it stays away and finally disappears. Thus it betrays how incapable it is of seeking and finding truth (II.ii.12; cf. II.ii.12-14, 18, 20).

In the 16th and 17th centuries there was a vigorous and often acrimonious dispute between Thomists and Calvinists as to the effects of sin on man's nature. The Calvinists held that sin had affected *all* our capacities, including our reason, so that we were "totally depraved." The Thomists insisted that sin had not affected man's reason *as such*. For it has not affected our *natural* capacities.

It is very difficult for us in the 20th century to put our finger on what exactly it was that the dispute was about. Calvin, after all, did not hold that in our state of sin we are natively more stupid than otherwise we would be, nor that our intelligence quotient is raised when we are freed from sin in faith. Nor did Thomas hold that sin has no effect on what we come to know. I suggest that the dispute was in large measure a (somewhat confused) dispute about preconditionalism. Whether the Calvinists, the defenders of preconditionalism, were also in opposition to the foundationalism of the Thomists is, I think, thoroughly unclear.

13. It is possible to have a foundationalist doctrine of warranted belief, as well as a foundationalist doctrine of warranted theory-acceptance. There are various possibilities. One is this: *One is warranted in believing p if and only if one is warranted in believing that p is justified by what could be apprehended with certitude.* Another is this: *One is warranted in believing p if and only if one is warranted in believing that someone has actually apprehended that p is justified by some proposition which has been apprehended with certitude.* A third is this: *One is warranted in believing p if and only if one remembers that one has oneself apprehended that p is justified by some proposition which one has apprehended with certitude.*

14. See P. Schilpp, *The Philosophy of Rudolf Carnap* (La Salle, Ill., 1962), p. 57.

15. Other relations than consistency may be specified. The general schema is this: *A theory T belongs to genuine science only if T bears the relation R to the foundation and someone could know with certitude that T bears R to the foundation.* Or rather, that is the schema appropriate to the Platonic concept of science. The schema appropriate to the progressive concept would be this: *A theory T belongs to genuine science at some time t only if T bears the relation R to the foundation and someone knows with certitude at or before t that T bears R to the foundation.* All of these, by making do with necessary *or* sufficient conditions, are *diminished* conditions for a theory's belonging to genuine science—diminished foundationalist conditions.

If we can get a necessary and sufficient condition for a theory's belonging to genuine science by adding some nonfoundational properties of theories to one or another instance of these formulas, then we still get a full-fledged criterion for theory acceptance. But it will be only a quasi-foundationalist criterion.

16. If one relaxes the search for a necessary and sufficient condition for warranted theory acceptance, and is content merely with one or another necessary, or sufficient, condition, then obviously there are many different versions of diminished foundationalism. Falsificationism is just one.

17. Quoted in Karl Popper, *The Logic of Scientific Discovery*

(London, 1959), p. 280.

18. See Imre Lakatos, *op. cit.,* pp. 100ff. Lakatos summarizes the situation neatly: *"Even if* there were a firmly established empirical basis to serve as launching pad for the arrow of *modus tollens,* the prime target remains hopelessly elusive" (p. 102).

19. This is what I contend in "Canon and Criterion," in *The Reformed Journal,* Oct. 1969.

20. This was Galileo's own solution. See his letter to the Grand Duchess Christina, reprinted in S. Drake (ed.), *Discoveries and Opinions of Galileo* (New York, 1957), pp. 173-216.

21. Lakatos, *op. cit.,* pp. 100f.

22. See R. Firth, "The Anatomy of Certainty," in *Philosophical Review,* 76 (1967); and William Alston, "Varieties of Privileged Access," in *American Philosophical Quarterly,* Vol. 8, No. 3 (July 1971). Also P. De Vos, "Certainty and the Method of Hyperbolic Doubt," in a forthcoming book on Descartes.

23. Presumably what is at issue here is not psychological inability to disbelieve. Perhaps we are sometimes (causally) unable to disbelieve something which in fact we would be warranted in disbelieving. But that is irrelevant. What is relevant, rather than such psychological inability, is just being warranted in disbelieving. We can put it together like this:

> x knows p indubitably $=_{df} x$ believes p; p is true; and it is impossible that p should be true and that x should have reasons for not believing p which, in conjunction with those he has for believing p, warrant him in not believing p.

24. We can put it thus:

> x knows p non-inferentially $=_{df} x$ knows p; and there is no other proposition q which x knows from which p can be inferred by satisfactory rules of inference, and which is such that if x didn't know q he wouldn't know p.

25. The aim of these sense-datum theorists was to find something that we do experience and about which we cannot be mistaken. Probably there are no such entities.

26. See my articles, "On God Speaking," "How God Speaks," and "Canon and Criterion," in *The Reformed Journal,* July-Aug., Sept., and Oct. 1969.

27. See George Mavrodes, "The Bible Buyer," in *The Reformed Journal,* July-Aug. 1968.

28. Because there are so many different actions we can and do

perform with respect to theories, both in and out of science, we shall henceforth avoid the terms "theorizing" and "theoretical activity," which tend to blur together a number of distinct activities.

Devising a theory obviously presupposes an act of *abstraction* on the part of the person who devises it. It presupposes that he has focused his attention on a certain limited range of some entities' properties or relations, to the ignoring of others. But it would be a mistake to conclude from this that abstraction is an identifying characteristic of the devising of theories, or even that it is an identifying characteristic of the devising of *scientific* theories. For one thing, abstractively attending to some limited range of some entities' properties or relations does not yet give one a theory— does not yet give one a generalization. But also, abstraction can occur when theories are not even in view. It occurs when, in listening to a musical work, I focus my attention on a certain limited range of the work's features and allow others to recede into the penumbra of my attention. Indeed, no one could, even if he wished, focus his attention on all the properties of the music that he is listening to.

It may well be that what differentiates one science from others is that it deals with only a certain limited range of the properties of those entities which fall within the scope of that science's theories. If so, then abstraction is at the basis of our differentiation of sciences. Yet it remains true that the devising of theories does not *consist in* the abstraction of properties, and that the abstracting of properties does not occur only in the devising of theories.

29. See Imre Lakatos, "Falsification and Scientific Research Programs," in Lakatos and Musgrave, *Criticism and the Growth of Knowledge* (Cambridge, 1970). See also Thomas Kuhn, *The Structure of Scientific Revolutions* (Chicago, 1962).

30. One can weigh a theory with respect to others of its features than this, for example, with respect to its aesthetic qualities—its elegance or inelegance.

31. Just what this last relation may be, that of *comporting as well as possible with,* I cannot explain. But it seems to me clear that often we demand more than logical consistency between theory and control belief; and it seems to me that sometimes at least that "more" can be aptly described with these words. Also, sometimes the situation is not so much that we *search for* a theory consistent or comportible with some control belief of ours. Rather, our control belief *suggests* such a theory to us. The searching is at a minimum.

32. Pp. 14f. About the first part of this passage Noam Chomsky remarks, in his review of the book (*New York Review of Books*, Dec. 30, 1971): "Surely the task of a scientific analysis is to discover the facts and explain them. Suppose that in fact the human brain operates by physical principles (perhaps now unknown) that provide for free choice, appropriate to situations but only marginally affected by environmental contingencies. The task of scientific analysis is not—as Skinner believes— to demonstrate that the conditions to which he restricts his attention fully determine human behavior, but rather to discover whether in fact they do (or whether they are at all significant), a very different matter. If they do not, as seems plausible, the task of a scientific analysis will be to clarify the issues and discover an intelligible explanatory theory that will deal with the actual facts." About the latter part of the passage Chomsky remarks "This is true enough, if indeed there are no mediating states that can be characterized by an abstract theory of mind, and if personalities, etc., are no more real than the jubilance of a falling body. But if the factual assumptions are false, then we certainly do need to try to discover what the perquisites of autonomous man really are."

For a somewhat different perspective on the function of what I call "control beliefs" in theoretical activity, see Gary Gutting, "A Defense of the Logic of Discovery," in *Philosophical Forum*, IV, 3. Gutting distinguishes between the logic of confirmation and the logic of discovery. He holds that *regulative principles* (as he calls them) function in the latter but not in the former. They function as premises in argument whose conclusions are of the form "It is plausible to think that T can be confirmed." My doubts that a satisfactory concept of confirmation can be framed have led me to pursue a different approach. I speak only about weighing a theory as to its acceptability, not about weighing a theory as to its promise for proving acceptable. And what I call *data beliefs* are, strictly speaking, a subset of what I call *control beliefs*. P's control beliefs for the weighing of theory T are beliefs of P which P requires T to be consistent with (or to comport well with) if he is to accept T. Among these will be certain singular propositions about the entities in T's scope. And these are P's data beliefs for his weighing of T. Among P's control beliefs for his weighing of T may of course be some belief to the effect that if T is to be accepted T ought to bear R to those beliefs which are data for weighing T—where R is a more stringent relation than just that of logical consistency.

33. Some very interesting points are made by James Barr in his discussion of what happens when a religious community which had previously possessed only an oral tradition establishes for

itself a canon of sacred *writings*. See his *The Bible in the Modern World* (New York, 1973), particulary pp. 127ff., 150ff.

34. I should explain why I use the word "commitment" when the word "faith" might have been expected. I have two reasons, somewhat connected. A point persuasively made by F. G. Downing in his *Has Christianity a Revelation?* is that the biblical writers relatively seldom speak about God revealing something. Much more often they speak about God *speaking*. And only on the rarest occasions do they speak about God revealing *himself.* So it seems to me that we should make *God speaking/man hearing* the basic structure of our theologies. Yet all the classical theologies have gone further and understood the revelation in question as consisting of God's self-revelation.

One might be inclined to respond that to speak of God revealing is to say the same thing in different words as to speak of God speaking. But that is false. The difference can perhaps best be seen by reflecting on human speech. Suppose I say to you "Close the door." No doubt in saying this I reveal various things, in particular, various things about myself. But I would regard it as perverse on your part for you to focus on that. For it was only in the course of *issuing a command* that I revealed something. And my intent in issuing the command was not to satisfy your curiosity about me, but to get you to close the door. Now it is because *faith* has always been paired off with *revelation* in the classical theologies, and because I think that God's speaking rather than God's revealing should be taken as our basic theological concept, that I wish to avoid using the concept of faith at this point.

Secondly, the biblical writers do of course use the concept of faith. But faith, as Paul uses the concept, does not cover the whole of the Christian's appropriate response to God. It is one among other Christian virtues. Of course one can redefine the word "faith" by attaching it to a concept which does cover the whole of the Christian life rather than just one of the Christian virtues. But that procedure seems to me rich with potential for confusion.

35. By a *proposition* I just mean something which can be asserted. Propositions are thus true or false. Cf. my *On Universals* (Chicago, 1970), Chap. I.

36. It may be added that the people's being called to speak and act and live in certain ways also presupposes the truth of various propositions which the people is not itself called, as part of its obedience, to believe. The people, for example, is called to tell of God's acts in history. And as I have argued elsewhere God can act in the described manner only if he is in time. Yet God's temporality

is probably not itself part of what God's people is called to believe, but only a presupposition thereof. See my "God Everlasting," in C. J. Orlebeke and L. B. Smedes (eds.), *God and the Good* (Grand Rapids, 1975).

37. The fact that the belief-content is not just about the supernatural is, in my judgment, an important factor in the Christian view as to the place of religion in American society. See my "Impartiality and Neutrality," in T. Sizer (ed.), *Religion and Public Education* (Boston, 1967).

38. It may even be that the belief-content of my authentic Christian commitment contains certain falsehoods. Frequently in teaching children one tells them what is, strictly speaking, false. So also it may be that some of what God says to us is, strictly speaking, false, accommodated to our frailty. Yet it may be that we are obliged to believe it.

It should be noticed that the belief-content of my authentic Christian commitment will differ from those beliefs which it is necessary for me to hold if I am to be a Christian at all. This latter is *minimally necessary* for being a Christian. The former is what is *maximally obligatory.*

39. Note that I do *not* say that he ought to allow the belief-content of his *actual* Christian commitment, but rather the belief-content of his *authentic* commitment, to control his devising and weighing of theories. For if the former diverges from the latter, then his prior obligation is to bring it into conformity with his *authentic* commitment.

40. To reject a theory is not necessarily to be done with it. Often when one is confronted with a theory he knows to be unacceptable, the best strategy is to pursue various research programs suggested by the theory, in the hope that along the way some clues will emerge for the construction of an alternative and better theory.

41. The point I make here has an interesting parallel in some remarks by Flannery O'Connor about the writing of short stories. She says: "Now this is a very humble level to have to begin on, and most people who think they want to write stories are not willing to start there. They want to write about problems, not people; or about abstract issues, not concrete situations. They have an idea, or a feeling, or an overflowing ego, or they want to Be A Writer, or they want to give their wisdom to the world in a simple enough way for the world to be able to absorb it. In any case, they don't have a story and they wouldn't be willing to write it if they did; and in the absence of a story, they set out to find a theory or a formula or a

technique. Now none of this is to say that when you write a story, you are supposed to forget or give up any moral position that you hold. Your beliefs will be the light by which you see, but they will not be what you see and they will not be a substitute for seeing." *Mystery and Manners* (New York, 1957), pp. 90f.

42. For an introduction to the issues see Peter Toon, "The Development of Doctrine," in *The Reformed Journal,* March 1973.

43. Of course this presupposes that none of his theological theories was taken from the belief-content of his assent in the first place.

44. Perhaps here is the place to take note of the common insistence that the biblical writings contain no theories, and that in this respect they differ from the writings of theologians. I think that the point usually being made by those who say this is that the biblical writings are not *disinterested.* They are always addressed to practical, religious problems; whereas the writings of theologians are generally disinterested, concerned just with the truth of the matter. As a rough-and-ready generalization this is probably true. But of course theories may be entertained either in interested or disinterested discourse. Thus I see no harm in saying that in St. Paul one finds theological theories (unless one defines a "theory" as something held tentatively, which I do not).

45. When one looks at Christian scholarship in the way I have sketched above it seems clear that *apologetics* (defense of the faith) is not some distinct area of inquiry to be assigned to theologians. The psychologist who rejects behaviorism and works out a psychological action-theory as an option to the pervasive behavior-theories should be viewed as, in effect, engaged in apologetics. Compare what Lakatos (*loc. cit.*) says concerning the construction of a "protective belt" for a scientific theory.

46. For a discussion of some historical examples of changes induced in people's actual commitment by developments in the sciences see Richard Popkin, "Scepticism, Theology and the Scientific Revolution in the Seventeenth Century," in Lakatos and Musgrave (eds.), *Philosophy of Science* (Amsterdam, 1968).

47. What often happens as part of this process is that a scholar is forced to *structure* the belief-content of his commitment in terms of what is more essential and what is less essential, what is nearer the core and what is nearer the periphery.

48. Some of these matters I have discussed in my "Canon and Criterion," in *The Reformed Journal,* Oct. 1969; see also the replies to letters in *The Reformed Journal,* March 1970.

49. In *Christian Letters To A Post-Christian World* (Grand Rapids, 1969), pp. 69ff.

Notes to Part II

1. Jürgen Habermas, *Knowledge and Human Interests* (Boston, 1971), pp. 301–2.

2. Some might question whether this justification can in fact be ascribed to the Pythagoreans. Not being a specialist in the intricacies of Pythagorean scholarship, the best I can do is cite authority. To the best of my knowledge, there is no fragment from the Pythagoreans which decisively offers the justification cited. Here, though, is what Kirk & Raven say in their interpretation of some of the fragments pertaining to Pythagoras: "The central notions, which held together the two strands that were later to fall apart, seem to have been those of θεωρία (contemplation), χόσμος (an orderliness found in the arrangement of the universe), and χάθαρσις (purification). By contemplating the principle of order revealed in the universe—and especially in the regular movements of the heavenly bodies—and by assimilating himself to that orderliness, man himself was progressively purified until he eventually escaped from the cycle of birth and attained immortality." G. S. Kirk & J. E. Raven, *The Presocratic Philosophers* (Cambridge, 1963), p. 228.

3. Augustine, *On the Trinity,* XII, 15.

4. Thomas Aquinas, *Summa Theologica,* IIa, Q. 66, Art. 5, *resp.* Hereafter, *ST.*

5. In recent years we have even seen a curious absorption of the Pythagorean tradition by the Baconian. The confidence was worn thin in our century that scholarship naturally tends toward self-improvement. To us it no longer seems that it tends naturally to improve our character. At the same time, however, our psychologists claim to have discovered laws concerning psychological self-alteration. And this has opened up the possibility of technologies for psychological self-improvement. Our technologists of self propose, for example, to teach us how to *express* our anger rather than suppress it. For it has been discovered, so they claim, that if one expresses one's anger, one will be a happier person.

6. There are other similar principles in the region here; for example: Choose those directions of inquiry which hold the greatest promise of yielding knowledge of greatest intrinsic worth

to *oneself.* It would overburden the text to canvass the various possibilities. What should also be observed is that the scholar operating with the principle in the text may find that he is confronted with great promise of gaining knowledge of moderate intrinsic worth and small promise of gaining knowledge of great intrinsic worth. Then he must weigh off the potential benefits of each option by a decision procedure. So too the scholar may be forced to choose between knowledge of lesser worth attainable by more people, and knowledge of greater worth attainable by fewer. Down through the ages, scholars have defended the latter choice by various notions of some vicarious benefit that mankind in general derives from the presence of the scholar in its midst.

7. In principle a scholar may have reasons of *both* sorts for following certain directions of inquiry. In such cases of coincidence, he will be engaged in both pure and praxis-oriented theory. Also, in following a given line of inquiry the scholar may be engaged in a mixture of pure and praxis-oriented theory.

8. The looseness to which I call attention between the justification offered for theory and the choice-principle used in determining the direction of one's theory is perhaps even more clear in the case of the Pythagorean justification. Neither on the ancient version of the Pythagorean tradition which Habermas describes nor on the modern variant to which I alluded does the interest which undergirds learning give the scholar any guidance in his decision as to which line of inquiry to pursue. It makes no difference whatsoever which facet of the cosmos's eternal order one contemplates; one's soul will be ordered nonetheless. It makes no difference whatsoever on which matters of inquiry one uses the scientific methodology; one's character will be purged. Yet the theorist must choose his direction of inquiry.

On this issue, the Renaissance humanists constituted an interestingly different version of the Pythagorean tradition from the ancients. At the heart of their program was a new vision of learning. In place of the formulation of theories characteristic of the schoolman, the humanist proposed the reading of classical texts and the study of classical history. He did not propose such hermeneutic/historical studies for the sake of the knowledge which would result. He proposed them for the sake of the results anticipated in the character of the scholar. Such studies, he thought, would make the scholar himself a cultured human being. And that was his ideal: The cultured man. Learning was for self-improvement. But the humanist was far indeed from thinking that every form of scholarly inquiry would produce the kind of self-improvement that he had in mind. He insisted that the theorizing of the schoolmen would not. Thus that particular justification which the humanists offered for learning yielded a principle of choice: Hermeneutic/historical studies will be chosen over scholastic theorizing. Whether this justification also yields a principle for choosing *within* the area of hermeneutic/historical studies is much less clear.

9. Other justifications can be offered for engaging in subjective pure theory than that the knowledge which results will somehow satisfy the Baconian justification. Someone might argue, for example, that just the satisfaction of intellectual curiosity is one of the things which is of inherent worth for human beings.

In this paper I do not at all try to state what, in general, makes some knowledge of greater inherent worth than other—though I assume that some is. Nor do I explore the connection between knowledge being of inherent worth, and the fact that someone or other finds that it's of intellectual interest. If satisfying one's intellectual interest is what gives knowledge inherent worth, then, given that intellectual interests vary, presumably which knowledge is of inherent worth also varies from one person to another. In any case, objective pure theory and subjective pure theory may not be such stark alternatives as the text above suggests. Still, we all sometimes have the experience of having an intense interest in acquiring some bit of knowledge which we judge unimportant and trivial—as in trying to solve some riddle or puzzle. Throughout our discussion we should also keep in mind the distinction between the state of *having* some item of knowledge and the experience of *acquiring* some item of knowledge. It seems to me that the contemporary scholar assigns relatively more weight to the latter than did the scholar in the tradition. Today we often prize the experience of acquiring knowledge more highly than the state of having it.

10. I am assuming that the principle *Choose whichever holds the greatest promise of yielding results or utility of greatest worth to the greatest number of people* will not necessarily coincide in its results with the principle *Choose whichever holds the greatest promise of yielding knowledge of greatest intrinsic worth to the greatest number of people.* For if it did, then of course the person who holds that some knowledge is of intrinsic worth could nonetheless use the principle formulated in the text. Likewise, I am assuming that the worth of the results or utility of knowledge will not always and necessarily outweigh the intrinsic worth of knowledge. For if it did, then again the person who holds that some knowledge is of intrinsic worth could nonetheless operate with the principle formulated in the text.

11. I am assuming that the intrinsic worth of knowledge will not always outweigh the worth of the inherent results or utility of knowledge. For if it did, then of course the theorist would never go wrong if he engaged solely in pure theory.

12. José Miguez-Bonino, *Doing Theology in a Revolutionary Situation* (Philadelphia, 1975), p. 88.

13. Though Augustine would add that it is only *deepened* knowledge which can come thus. The beginning lies in faith.

14. Compare these perceptive words of Miguez-Bonino: "The faith of Israel is consistently portrayed, not as a *gnosis,* but as a *way,* a particular way of acting, of relating inside and outside the nation, or ordering life at every conceivable level, which corresponds to God's own way with Israel. This background, so well attested in the Psalms, for instance, may explain Jesus' use of the word *way* to refer to himself. The motif, on the other hand, appears in parenetic contexts in Pauline literature. Faith is a 'walking.' It is unnecessary to point out that even the idea of knowledge and knowing has this active and participatory content." *Doing Theology,* p. 89.

15. *Summa Theologica;* Part IIA, Q. 3, Art. 3, *resp.*

16. *ST,* Part IIB, Q. 23, Art. 8, *resp.*

17. *ST,* Part IIA, Q. 3, Art. 4, *resp.*

18. *ST,* Part IIA, Q. 3, Art. 8, *resp.*

19. *ST,* Part IIA, Q. 3, Art. 4, *resp.*

20. *ST,* Part IIA, Q. 3, Art. 5, *resp.*

21. *ST,* Part IIA, Q. 5, Art. 3, *resp.*

22. *Summa contra Gentiles,* I, 2. Hereafter, *SCG.*

23. *ST,* IIB, Q. 23, Art. 1, *resp.*

24. *ST,* IIB, Q. 23, Art. 3, *resp.*

25. *ST,* IIB, Q. 26, Art. 2, *obj.* 2.

26. *SCG,* I, 2.

27. *ST,* IIA, Q. 4, Art. 8; and *ST,* IIA, Q. 4, Art. 3.

28. *ST,* IIA, Q. 4, Art. 8, *resp.*

29. Ibid.

30. *ST,* IIA, Q. 4, Art. 3, *resp.*

31. Ibid.

32. *ST,* IIA, Q. 4, Art. 7, *resp.*

33. Miguez-Bonino's phrase in *Doing Theology,* p. 91.